Altars
OF THE HEART

Healing Wounded Emotions
in the Presence of God

THOM GARDNER

Treasure House

An Imprint of

Destiny Image® Publishers, Inc.
P.O. Box 310
Shippensburg, PA 17257-0310

"For where your treasure is, there will your heart be also."
Matthew 6:21

ISBN 0-7684-3009-7

For Worldwide Distribution
Printed in the U.S.A.

This book and all other Destiny Image, Revival Press, MercyPlace, Fresh Bread, Destiny Image Fiction, and Treasure House books are available at Christian bookstores and distributors worldwide.

For a U.S. bookstore nearest you, call **1-800-722-6774**.
For more information on foreign distributors, call **717-532-3040**.
Or reach us on the Internet:

www.destinyimage.com

CONTENTS

AUTHOR'S PREFACE

This book is intended to be used as a personal study that leads to the healing of wounded emotions and brings the reader into a greater intimacy with God. It is not a training manual by itself for facilitation of inner healing. Readers with serious life-controlling emotional issues should not rely on this book alone for healing, but should seek out additional competent help from others who have been trained in the ministry of inner healing.

You will note that I have borrowed some terms from Theophostic Ministry, which was developed by Ed Smith, along with other terms that have been common to the ministry of inner healing for many years.

This book includes a reference list for further study. I encourage those who want to administer inner healing to seek thorough training through Grace and Truth Fellowship, Inc., which provides local churches with basic training in the ministry of inner healing (www.GraceandTruth.us / 717-263-6869), or Theophostic Ministries (www.theophostic.com / 270-465-3757) or Cornerstone Bible Institute and Seminary (www.Cornerstonenet.org / 540-432-2355) or some other recognized source of equipping in the ministry of inner healing. Cornerstone Seminary has a complete track of study on inner healing, featuring classes on Communion with God, Renewing the Mind, and Prayer Counseling.

There are many different approaches to inner healing available throughout the Body of Christ. None of the ones listed above represent the only way to find healing in the presence of God.

It is my desire to see you healed and whole, living in the abundant life to which you have been called through Jesus Christ.

FOREWORD

Most of us spend a considerable portion of our adult lives trying to come to terms with what happened to us in the past. Our prayers, our repentance, and our desires all seem to focus on what life would be like if only "that incident" would not have happened, or if only that gaping emotional wound in our heart could be healed once and for all. But this kind of living must come to an end. If we truly desire a serious and continuous growth in our walk with the Lord, we must realize that dragging around all that stuff from our past eventually becomes too much to bear, too much to keep track of, and definitely too much to fit into God's plan for our lives.

Trying to survive, we have discovered a hundred ways to cover the pain and ignore the haunting images and feelings that follow us everywhere we try to live. We've tried painting them over with religious activity. We've tried to deny them by anesthetizing ourselves with new highs of emotion. We've tried to rebuke them, cast them out, pray them away, sing and dance them away. But when the music was over, when the lights were turned off, we found ourselves hurting with the same intensity as before, wondering if there really would be healing for the things that happened so long ago.

I understand. It is not that we try to ignore the pain. Certainly, it is often so intense that it consumes us as though it happened today. It is not as though we try to cover it. The pain has been too hard for too long. We know better. The pain is there even with a cover over it. We have tried that way out. It is not that we try to deny that it exists or deny that the event ever happened. Repentance seems to be a minute-by-minute experience. We are totally aware of what we suffer.

But when the sense of His calling to us is greater than the pain, when the hope of His presence draws us forward stronger than our pain draws us backward, we make that decision that somehow, somewhere, this has got to end.

And so it can.

There is a place of healing in the Spirit of God, in the personal reality of His presence, that the Lord yearns for us to experience. He sees our pain, understands our struggle, and wants nothing more than to bring inner wholeness to His people, to you. This is the genuine place of healing.

Altars of the Heart gives us a biblical and simple approach to use in finding healing for those past hurts. Born out of the author's experience of ministering to thousands around the world, this book has answers, real answers, because it offers healing to the hurting believer.

There is a place of quietness in the heart of God where oil and wine are applied to our hurts.

There is healing in the presence of God.

Don Nori, Publisher
Author, *Secrets of the Most Holy Place*
and *Romancing the Divine*

INTRODUCTION

If you've picked up this book, there is a good chance you have some kind of emotional pain in your life. You may be a housewife who lives in secret dissatisfaction, wondering who you are now that the kids have grown up. Maybe you're the preacher who struggles to feel something, who keeps going because you have to—it *is* expected, after all. You could be the homecoming queen who seems to have everything, yet is locked in a battle for approval.

Each of us has some kind of limp in our step as we walk through daily life. We get up in the morning and the limp is not too noticeable; kind of like the limp we might have with a small pebble in our shoe. Then we go to the office and our gait becomes a little stiffer—the pebble has gotten a little bigger and our limp a little more pronounced as we have encountered various issues and conflicts. Maybe we go to our Bible study in the evening and leave feeling more guilty and depressed than when we got there. By the time we get home and throw ourselves into bed, we can hardly walk. The small pebble that was in our shoe in the morning has grown all day and become a boulder. Something has a hold on us—something has compromised our walk.

What are these things that make us limp? They are false beliefs that come up time and time again, like that pebble stuck in our shoe, telling us how to live and where to go. They determine how we live and walk and how we interpret the world around us. They are so much a part of us that we can't remember a time when we didn't limp. Soon we limp without knowing why—it has become automatic.

I remember a story my wife told me about a dog she had when she was younger. Her father once stepped on the dog's paw by accident and, although the dog was not seriously hurt, it occasionally limped as if to elicit sympathy from people by reminding them of what had been done to it in the past. In fact, it would sometimes favor the wrong paw. That dog limped when there seemed to be no real reason, just because of something that had happened long before—which is often exactly what we do.

I've written this book to address the limps in our lives. I have included several instances and illustrations from the lives of the wonderful folks I have ministered to and with—changing the names and specific details, of course, to maintain anonymity. Nevertheless, they are *real* people with *real* problems who have since experienced *real* healing and freedom in Christ.

Many books have been written on the healing of wounded emotions, and I have read and profited from many of them through the years. I have also been the beneficiary of some great teaching by a mentor of mine, Pastor Roy Kreider, who spoke the words of life to me that launched my full-time ministry in healing wounded emotions. I have also listened to and been influenced by the teaching of Dr. Ed Smith, whose breakthrough in Theophostic Ministry has brought healing and peace to hundreds of thousands. I also appreciate the teaching and ministry of John and Paula Sandford, who have given much in the realm of inner healing and deliverance. All of these people have added immeasurably to my understanding and personal healing. I appreciate all of them and pray that this humble book will complement their teachings.

So why write another book on inner healing? *Altars of the Heart* does not just present another method for healing. It is based primarily on the exposition of Deuteronomy 7:1-7, which I preached about several years ago, and which the Lord has added much to. The ideas presented are similar to those in other approaches to healing. However, my primary motive for writing this book is to provide a biblical format through which the wounded are brought into an awareness of the presence of God, which enables them to destroy lies and false images by following a simple biblical process.

This is not a psychology book, nor is it science or a new form of Christian counseling. In fact, it is not a counseling book at all. It is based upon biblical exposition and practical experience gained while ministering healing in a way that focuses on the presence of God, who is the source of all healing. This book exists to provide an opportunity for people to find healing for wounds and limping limitations through a personal encounter with the exalted Christ. This material is also derived from the basic text for our inner healing training seminar called *Altars of the Heart Ministry Training Seminar*, which has now been offered in many parts of the country to train ministers to bring others into the presence of God for healing.

The Bible identifies seven basic influences in Deuteronomy chapter 7, as well as a host of negative emotions that flow from the lies, all of which compromise our inner peace. You will see these basic lies and emotional sets as they affected the lives of regular people in the Bible. Then you will have the opportunity to compare your life to theirs and find the source of the hurt that causes your limping today.

I ask you to read this book in the gentle tone in which it was written. This is not a book of shouting, but one of whispering in the presence of God—the Lord Himself who is our Healer (see Ex. 15:26).

Behold, I will bring to it health and healing, and I will heal them; and I will reveal to them an abundance of peace and truth (Jeremiah 33:6).

Part I

THE NEED FOR HEALING
WOUNDED EMOTIONS

Chapter One

A Fuller Gospel

When the Lord your God brings you into the land where you are entering to possess it... (Deuteronomy 7:1).

At no other time does our relationship with God show up more accurately than on Monday morning, the day after we are in church. Most of us attend Sunday morning services filled with beautiful music that prepares the way for some kind of thought-provoking teaching. And all of it transpires in the ambiance of spiritual brothers and sisters who smile at us in the warmth and generosity of Christian concern and comfort. As the service concludes, we are sure that we have heard or felt something from God that day. We believe we are inoculated for the rest of the week against the disease of despair.

However, the peace that seemed to blanket us in the presence of God begins to wane with the final strains of music as we stroll out the door and get into our vehicle. A strange empty feeling follows us as we walk through the rest of the day and order the events of the coming week. We don't think too much of it, though; this is the routine that we have followed for years—Sunday after Sunday, meeting after meeting, Bible study after Bible study. But what is this emptiness we feel?

On Monday morning we awaken with the novocaine of religious ecstasy having worn off, and we face life feeling emotionally naked and alone. A helpless, pointless, numb feeling carries us through the days and events of our routine. Our lives seem to waver between terror and tedium as we walk through our days in a kind of emotional fog that never allows us to see or discern objectively. In one sense it is like someone is riding on our backs and sinking his spurs in us to drive us by some kind of pain. We live fenced in by feelings we cannot explain and dare not discuss on Sunday, for to do so would be to incur the disdain of the righteous. Nothing is ever supposed to be wrong in our lives. We are Christians, after all!

Nevertheless, we wake up on Monday morning the same way that many do who do not call themselves Christians. This same reality surrounds those who don't go to church—those who don't call themselves Christians. They feel the same emptiness and controlling emotional spurs. They may have found some solace in their work or in some kind of New Age spiritual transcendence, but they feel the same way Monday that we do. They, as well as we, ask the same question: "Is this all there is?"

Many Christians are hounded by fear, rejection, worthlessness, shame, insecurity, defilement, hopelessness, or some combination of all of these. We may have a "saving knowledge" that we are bound for Heaven, but at the same time we live out a kind of emotional hell on earth. Many in the Body of Christ have yet to experience their "rebirthright" in Jesus Christ. Although we *should* be living in the power and purpose of God, we instead limp from one day to the next waiting to go to Heaven. That is *not* God's idea. This is *not* all there is to life on earth. Why do we live so far below our position in Christ? The truth is that while we may know the gospel, we have yet to *believe* it!

A Fuller Gospel

There is a "fuller gospel" than the one we have believed. The real good news is that God desires to "bring us into" a life of abundance in Christ. Jesus told us that He came so you and I "may have life, and have it abundantly" (Jn. 10:10b). He wants to take us beyond our emotional pain and limping limitations to a place characterized by the unconditional *love* and *acceptance* that we all long for and seldom realize. It is a place of peace and rest from the torment of satanically inspired lies that rob us of intimacy with God.

The greatest emotional struggles we experience are the result of our lack of understanding the simple truth that by His grace, God "hath made us accepted in the beloved [Jesus Christ]" (Eph. 1:6 KJV). This simple understanding could eliminate all of the emotional pain we suffer. The one thing that we all are looking for is a Father who will never abandon us or leave us alone. Thus the presence of God is the source of all healing. It is really what we all long for.

The apostle Paul understood how gloriously God met this most basic need of all people. Listen to his ecstatic praise in his letter to the Ephesians.

*Blessed be the God and Father of our Lord Jesus Christ, who hath blessed us with all spiritual blessings in heavenly places in Christ: according as He hath **chosen** us in Him before the foundation of the world, that we should be holy and without blame before Him in love: having predestinated us unto the **adoption** of children by Jesus Christ to Himself, according to the good pleasure of His will, to the praise of the glory of His grace, wherein He hath made us **accepted** in the beloved* (Ephesians 1:3-6 KJV).

Look at the key words in these verses. We are *chosen* and *loved* or *accepted* by God's will. That is the very description of the term *adoption* that Paul used so many times throughout the Epistles. When a couple adopts a baby, they are *choosing* a child to *love*. God is no different. In fact, God has not gone through the orphanage with a list of expectations and descriptions looking for perfect children. Rather, God picked us up as we lay in our dirty diapers with the sole intention of loving us, and He will never put us down again! He has chosen us and loved us "to the praise of the glory of His grace"! God has *chosen* us and *loved* us simply because He desires to do so. How much of our pain could be alleviated—how many of our wounds healed—if we could truly experience and believe this astounding and irrational love of God?

God has always desired to express His love for man. In the Torah, God moved the nation of Israel toward a "homeland" where His love and acceptance would be the rule of life. It was the thought of this homeland that captivated the life of Abraham, who "by faith...lived as an alien in the land of promise, as in a foreign land, dwelling in tents with Isaac and Jacob, fellow heirs of the same promise; for he was looking for the city which has foundations, whose architect and builder is God" (Heb. 11:9-10). God promised Abraham a home—an inheritance that God would secure by His own faithfulness (see Gen. 15)—and the only requirement was that Abraham would trust God to do it. We today have entered into the same promises God made to Abraham by the blood of Christ. And God also is moving us toward this place that feels like home, or at least feels like the way home should feel.

Dr. Larry Crabb, who wrote *Effective Biblical Counseling*, refers to these two primary needs of love and acceptance as the needs for "security" and "significance." These became needs as a result of our broken relationship with God. Dr. Crabb says,

"I believe that at the fall Adam and Eve were both significant and secure. From the moment of their creation their needs were fully met in a relationship with God unmarred by sin. Significance and security were attributes of qualities already resident in their personalities, so they never gave them a second thought. When sin ended their innocence and broke their relationship with God, what formerly were attributes became needs."[1]

We are "secure" in the *love* of God and "significant" in that God has *chosen* us. There can be no higher significance than to be chosen by the One who created us. Apart from our understanding that we are chosen or accepted by God, we will try all manner of things to achieve acceptability, most of which will end up wounding us further. On the other hand, out of the love and acceptance of God comes all that we could ever want or need for a whole and meaningful life. And that is where God is taking us—that is what He desires to "bring us into."

What Life Was Meant to Be

As we read the biblical narrative of creation, we see that God's design for us was simple (see Gen. 1:27-28; 2:7-8,15). God's desire was communion with man, and all of man's needs would be met entirely in his communion with God. For a time, man lived in the pure and unadulterated truth of God's love and acceptance and enjoyed emotional wholeness. There was no fear, no rejection, no unworthiness—only total trust in an atmosphere of truth and purposeful intimacy. This was what God meant life to be for all of us. Alas, man succumbed to the lies of the serpent and became separated from God in sin. (We will discuss this more fully in the next chapter.)

In Deuteronomy 7:7 Moses tells Israel that "the Lord did not set His love on you nor choose you because you were more in number than any of the peoples, for you were the fewest of all peoples." In other words, God did not offer them love and acceptance because of anything they did or deserved, but simply out of His own nature and desire for intimate fellowship. The place into which God was leading Israel in Deuteronomy 7

---

1.   Dr. Larry Crabb, *Effective Biblical Counseling* (Grand Rapids, MI: Zondervan Publishing House, 1977), p. 61.

was an Old Testament example of the place where God now is leading those who are in Christ.

The "land" that is spoken of in Deuteronomy 7 typifies a place of intimate communion between God and His people where all that was lost in Eden would be restored. There would be no more fear or separation from God, and every facet of man's life would be wrapped up and lived in the presence of God. God in Christ has brought us into this place, though few have entered into it fully.

Out of God's love and acceptance for His people Israel flowed all that was necessary for their life and prosperity. God brought them into a land of "cities which you did not build, and houses full of all good things which you did not fill, and hewn cisterns which you did not dig," and "vineyards and olive trees which you did not plant" (Deut. 6:10-11). In other words, they were to experience the "riches of His grace" just as Paul mentioned in Ephesians 1:7. All that the Israelites would have or achieve would be a by-product of the grace of a loving Father and the intimacy He restored.

The Bible describes this "grace-land" in several ways. Let's look briefly at a few of them, for each points to something that we should be experiencing today as children of God in Christ Jesus.

Rest and Peace

It was to be a land "flowing with milk and honey" (Deut. 6:3). When our daughters were babies and refused to fall asleep, my wife used an Old World sedative that worked every time. As the girls lay fidgeting in their beds, Carol would heat up some milk and add some honey to it. After our daughters took a few sips of nature's sleeping potion, they always would fall asleep. It was a surefire way to still even the greatest upheaval of the day. The taste of milk and honey meant love to our children. I wish sometimes that I could recapture but a snapshot of that restful sleep that used to come across the faces of our little ones as they lay in bed. When I think of a "land flowing with milk and honey," I envision a place of rest and peace. This *rest* and *peace* are the result of dwelling in God's love and acceptance.

Note that the Bible says it was a land "flowing" with milk and honey. It was not just trickling; it was flowing. There was no scarcity of supply—no fear that anyone would lack provision. This new homeland was the place where fear and want would be totally dispatched in favor of God's *abundance*.

Today Christ has *become* our peace (see Eph. 2:14). But how many of us really live in the peace and rest that Christ has provided at the cost of His own blood? Many fidget and squirm in the lap of God. Many could use a sip of the real milk and honey of Christ's peace. If we are not experiencing that peace in our lives, God wants to bring us into a new place of understanding of the truth that brings peace.

Communion with God

The land into which Israel was being led was a place of communion with God—a place of intimate fellowship where God would be involved and acknowledged in every phase of life. God Himself told the nation many times of His desire to enjoy intimate communion with them.

> *I will give to you and to your descendants after you, the land of your sojournings, all the land of Canaan, for an everlasting possession; and I will be their God* (Genesis 17:8).

> *I will also walk among you and be your God, and you shall be My people* (Leviticus 26:12).

> *Let them construct a sanctuary for Me, that I may dwell among them* (Exodus 25:8).

> *I will dwell among the sons of Israel and will be their God* (Exodus 29:45).

Communion was foremost in God's heart as He prepared the nation of Israel to cross over into the land of grace. Intimate communion is God's plan for us as well. In Christ God brought all mankind back into this relationship of intimate communion—a purposeful intimacy where all that man was and all that he did flowed from his oneness with God. Jesus said, "If anyone loves Me, he will keep My word; and My Father will love him, and We will come to him and make Our abode [have communion] with him" (Jn. 14:23). In other words, obedience and purpose flows out of our intimacy with God. It is God's desire that we experience His presence and involvement in every facet of our lives. All that God has done for us in Christ leads to this intimate relationship.

Purpose and Worth

God also intended the nation of Israel to derive their purpose and worth from their unique relationship with Him. In fact, it was their relationship with God that set them apart from all other people on earth. Moses says, "For how then can it be known that I have found favor in Your sight, I and Your people? Is it not by Your going with us, so that we, I and Your people, may be distinguished from all the other people who are upon the face of the earth?" (Ex. 33:16) It was God's "going with" Israel—His presence among them—that gave them their "distinguishing" purpose and worth. So it is for us who are in Christ. It is our relationship with Christ that distinguishes us from all others. It is our position in Christ that determines our worth and purpose.

We live in a time when people wander from place to place searching for purpose and meaning in their lives. Recently I was in the great city of London, England. One evening I decided to set out on my own to walk a bit in the streets and look at the people. As I walked, I encountered people from many nations speaking several languages. They were all so different, yet they were all the same. They all had a look of aimlessness. They talked, shopped, and ate as if waiting for something to happen. They were going nowhere, and I'm sure that most arrived at that destination. As I looked into their eyes, I saw that life seemed to be a meaningless syncopation of events and purposeless wanderings for them.

The world assigns us our worth based on how much money we make or the titles and influence we hold, but our worth cannot be measured in dollars. Our true purpose and worth stem from our relationship with God. We are what we are by the grace of God. Those in Christ exist for the purpose of fellowship with God, giving Him glory through their lives. While the world works to *gain* acceptance, those in Christ work *because* of their acceptance in Christ.

God's plan for us is peace, rest, communion, purpose, and worth, and we obtain all of these "in Christ."

Taking Us into the Land

God has already prepared for us a place of wholeness where we have been chosen and loved in Christ. All of the things we discussed and much more are ours in Christ. He has become our inheritance. Many of us never experience the rest, peace, communion, purpose, and worth that are ours in Christ. We are tormented by negative emotions of fear, shame, and all the rest. However, in Christ we are chosen and loved, and it is out of this reality that our emotions are healed.

The presence of God demonstrates His healing power and reassurance of His love.

- When we feel fear…   Christ is with us.
- When we feel rejected…   Christ accepts us.
- When we feel worthless… Christ approves us.
- When we feel shame…   Christ covers us.
- When we feel insecure…   Christ surrounds us.
- When we feel defiled…   Christ restores us.
- When we feel hopeless…   Christ becomes our living hope.

We must realize that there is an active and deliberate plan devised to keep us from experiencing all of these benefits in Christ. Our common enemy cannot do anything to affect our salvation through Christ, but he will do his best to keep us from entering the rest and communion that is ours by Christ's own blood. There are great riches for us—a table of blessings to which we have been called. It is a table of chosenness and love under the grace of a loving Father.

So let us know, let us press on to know the Lord. His going forth is as certain as the dawn; and He will come to us like the rain, like the spring rain watering the earth (Hosea 6:3).

Chapter Two

LIVING THE LIES THAT BIND

...and clears away many nations before you, the Hittites and the Girgashites and the Amorites and the Canaanites and the Perizzites and the Hivites and the Jebusites, seven nations greater and stronger than you (Deuteronomy 7:1).

One afternoon my wife Carol and I were ministering to a couple in our congregation. Throughout the ministry session I saw Carol crying several times. I thought, *Wow. She is really into this session—really pouring herself out to the Lord for this couple.* But when the ministry time was over and we were leaving, the tears didn't stop. In fact, they intensified as we got in the car. It was pretty obvious, even to me, that something was happening inside Carol's heart. I didn't know what, though, so I asked her what was happening.

She replied that during the session when I read these verses from Psalm 139, "For You formed my inward parts; You wove me in my mother's womb. I will give thanks to You, for I am fearfully and wonderfully made; wonderful are Your works, and my soul knows it very well" (Ps. 139:13-14), the words triggered something in her. She didn't believe she was very wonderfully made. In fact, she saw herself as never able to do anything well. In short, she believed a lie.

When we got home we prayed that the Lord would reveal the source of this lie to her. In response, the Lord escorted Carol to a memory picture[2] of her third-grade classroom. One day a little girl who was partially blind came into the class, and Carol's teacher asked her to look after her. Needless to say, Carol was feeling pretty special about her assignment. It was a gesture of approval from her teacher. But it soon came crashing down—along with her confidence.

---

2. "Memory picture" is a term used by Theophostic Ministry. See *Beyond Tolerable Recovery*, Edward M. Smith, page 41. Also see comments on "reframing" memories from *Inner Healing* by Mike Flynn and Doug Gregg, pages 82-83.

Sometime after lunch, Carol's teacher came to her and said, "I think we'd better let someone else help this little girl." My wife did not hear or remember any reason why she should not continue to help this little girl. All she heard was that she was not able to do it to suit the teacher. She was devastated—humiliated. There was this picture of Carol as a little third-grade child sadly slumped over her desk coloring in a book, alone. What she felt was that she was not good enough to take care of the new girl—that there must have been something wrong with her. Because of this and other similar experiences, Carol grew up with a feeling of inadequacy. She lacked the confidence needed in order to follow through with good ideas. She only heard an inner voice telling her, "You can't do this" or "You're not good enough for that."

When we asked the Lord to reveal to her the truth as opposed to the lie, Carol saw our own daughter, Coco, sitting at a desk instead of her. (Carol is a schoolteacher and had both of her daughters in class, so the scene was not a stretch.) As we prayed, the presence of the Lord seemed to pour into the memory picture and a question arose from the midst of the scene. The Lord asked Carol, "How do you feel about this little girl?" Carol said, "I love her; I delight in her." The Lord responded, "And I delight in you!" Just then the feeling of worthlessness dissipated. Carol knew at last from the heart of God how He felt about her. And she believed it.

In the following months, Carol began to pursue the formation of a new drama department at the Christian school where she teaches—something she could never have done before because of a lack of confidence. The Lord led her to put on a production of "The Miracle Worker" throughout which she wove the words of Psalm 139 and the truth that God had brought her out of the darkness and into the light—that she was wonderfully made by the hand of God. Hundreds of people got to see the result of that healing truth as we wept at the healing grace of God.

This story demonstrates the usual course that the ministry of inner healing takes. When we learn the truth, it overcomes the lies we believe about God and ourselves and restores us to intimacy with God. Although Carol was obviously a talented and anointed woman, she believed and lived under the power of the lie that she could never do anything well enough. The comments and disapproval of her third-grade teacher eroded her confidence. Carol, like many of us, was living a lie—a lie that denies the truth about us and about the love and acceptance that is ours in

Christ. Her healing, and ours, comes as we experience the truth of who we are in Christ.

The Truth about Truth

If we are going to uncover the lies that bind us, we first need to know about truth. In order to receive truth and healing for our emotional wounds, we must understand what the truth is. I don't want to engage in philosophical questions about the nature of truth, although that can be a fascinating discussion. Instead, I want to state what truth is in its biblical definition.

Truth Is What Is True

Simply put, truth is what is real, and what is real is what comes of God. The Hebrew word for truth is *'emet*, which comes from the same word that we know as *amen*. *'Emet* refers to something that is true in its essence; it is faithful, real, dependable, and powerful. When we hear something that registers with us as trustworthy, we say "Amen!" The New Testament word is *alethia*, which again refers to something that is true or real versus what is false. Conversely, what is untrue is also unfaithful, un- real, undependable, and powerless—unless we empower it by believing it.

Another way to describe truth is to say that truth, insofar as God is concerned, is that which is whole or in order. When God speaks truth, the result is order. He spoke a word, and worlds came into being. Psalm 33:6 says that He spoke the heavens into existence. Whatever God speaks brings order and the resulting peace or wholeness. This is the Hebrew concept of *shalom*, which is a state of wholeness or integrity. Christ was *shalom* incarnate bringing truth, order, and peace to the earth. When the angels announced the birth to the shepherds, they announced that peace was "on earth"; they were proclaiming that order was being restored. The sequence then is truth, which restores order, which then results in peace with God. This is the same process that brings wholeness and peace in our individual lives. We must be put back in order to find emotional wholeness. And we must hear the truth if we are to be put back in order.

The opposite is also true. That which is untrue is out of order. When people wound us in some way, they have in effect spoken or done some- thing that is against the order or the truth of God. They leave us out of order and without peace. When children hear that they are lazy or stupid or perhaps suffer the pain of sexual abuse, they believe something that is not true, and as a result they order their lives around lies. The truth is that they are precious creations of God, but the lies they believe as a result of wounding leave them "out of order" and living under feelings of worthlessness or shame, which limit and control their lives.

When I was a child, we used to build "houses" with dominos or cards. But if just one of those dominos or cards was taken away, the whole structure would collapse. It is the same with truth. If something is untrue in the slightest way, the whole thing collapses in untruth. It takes only a little lie to cause a life to come crashing to the ground.

On the other hand, whatever God says is entirely true; it is in order. His Word is true; therefore, it has true power and effect. God speaks something and, since He is the ultimate Truth, whatever He says becomes true as well. God spoke the world into existence. "Then God said, 'Let there be light'; and there was light" (Gen. 1:3). The universe is *ordered* through God's word. What is not based on God's truth is out of order. Healing comes as we hear and experience the truth of God, which restores God's order in us. When we receive truth, our beliefs are reordered and, with them, our emotions.

Christ Is the Truth

Jesus Christ was Himself the very incarnation of the truth of God. Jesus said, "I am the way, and the truth, and the life; no one comes to the Father but through Me" (Jn. 14:6). The Gospel of John says that Jesus was "full of grace and truth" and that Jesus has "explained" or demonstrated the truth about God's intention toward man.

> *And the Word became flesh, and dwelt among us, and we saw His glory, glory as of the only begotten from the Father, **full of grace and truth**. John testified about Him and cried out, saying, "This was He of whom I said, 'He who comes after me has a higher rank than I, for He existed before me.' " For of His fullness we have all received, and grace upon grace. For the Law was given through Moses; grace and truth were realized through Jesus Christ. No one has seen God at any time; the only begotten God who is in the bosom of the Father, He has explained Him* (John 1:14-18).

Jesus is the true expression of all that is God. He is the "exact representation" of God's heart toward us in that He came to reconcile and restore us to God (Heb. 1:3). Truth is not a collection of facts no matter how well supported and obvious. Rather, truth is personified in Jesus Christ. So then we know if something is true by whether or not it sounds like Jesus. (We will discuss more about the sound of truth in a later chapter.)

The Origin of Lies

Just as truth has a source—God—so do the lies we believe have an original source. Jesus calls this source the "father of lies" and said that he was that way from the very beginning (Jn. 8:44). The lies and deception that we believe and live under are the product of a deliberate and diabolical plan to keep us separated from God. Into the Garden slithered the source and inspiration of all lies in the form of a serpent.

Now the serpent was more crafty than any beast of the field which the Lord God had made. And he said to the woman, "Indeed, has God said, 'You shall not eat from any tree of the garden'?" The woman said to the serpent, "From the fruit of the trees of the garden we may eat; but from the fruit of the tree which is in the middle of the garden, God has said, 'You shall not eat from it or touch it, or you will die.'" The serpent said to the woman, "You surely will not die! For God knows that in the day you eat from it your eyes will be opened, and you will be like God, knowing good and evil" (Genesis 3:1-5).

Satan's plan was to disrupt the union between God and man, to call God's unconditional love and acceptance into question. Satan brought disorder into the world by asking, in effect, "Did God really say that you couldn't eat from this tree?" He was implying that God was somehow less loving than man might have believed. How could a loving God deny us anything? Then he added, "God knows that when you eat this fruit you will become like Him, knowing good and evil." Satan implied that God was holding out on man—that man could better serve his own purpose instead of God's. It is the grandfather of all life-sapping lies: "You can be like God...." For the first time, man was presented with the idea that he could live separated from God. The result was tragic.

When man believed the lie and ate from the tree of the knowledge of good and evil, his eyes were opened and he was separated from the life of God, the blessing of God, the purpose of God, and communion with God. Sin entered the world, leaving man hiding behind his man-made apron of fig leaves. But God, who is rich in mercy, came looking for man: "Adam, where are you?" Obviously God knew what man had done, but both then and now, God is more concerned with where we are than what we've done, and He calls us back to intimacy.

In the wake of man's separation from God, all that he enjoyed as part of the intimate fellowship with God was subverted by opposites. Unconditional love and acceptance were replaced by fear and shame. Open and intimate fellowship with God gave way to hiding behind fig leaves and bushes. This is not God's plan or desire for any of us.

There is a host of lies that rob us of intimacy with God and cause us to live in our own strength separate from God. If we want to live in grace and emotional wholeness, we must uncover the lies we believe and subject them to the truth of God. The path the Israelites took to enter the Promised Land gives us some clues to these lies.

Greater and Stronger Influences

As Israel was about to cross into the inheritance of God, Moses warned them that they were going to encounter seven nations that were "greater and stronger" than they (Deut. 7:1). These influences would be obstacles to their enjoying the kind of abundance and intimacy with God that He intended. The following lists some of the negative emotions these ungodly nations suggest.

Hittites:	*Fear*
Girgashites:	*Rejection*
Amorites:	*Worthlessness*
Canaanites:	*Shame*
Perizzites:	*Insecurity*
Hivites:	*Defilement*
Jebusites:	*Hopelessness*

The names of each of these pagan nations suggest a strong influence that inhabited the land of grace and abundance into which God was bringing His people Israel.[3] The negative, emotional influences that these

---

3.   Compare these various influences with the categories of lies listed in *Beyond Tolerable Recovery*, pages 86-89. Also see *Deep Wounds, Deep Healing* by Charles H. Kraft, pages 183-188; and *Healing of Memories* by David A. Seamands, page 144.

names suggest still inhabit the abundant life that you and I were promised. Jesus said, "I came that they may have life, and have it abundantly" (Jn. 10:10b). He was comparing the kind of life He came to bring with the kind of life inspired by the thief who comes to steal, kill, and destroy us. The devil is the thief, and he is the father of lies (see Jn. 8:44; 10:10a). He inspires fear, rejection, shame, and all the rest. The kind of life Jesus meant for us is not one controlled by lies, nagging fears, and limiting thoughts, but one of wholeness. This whole life is one that is lived in the understanding that we are loved and chosen by God in Christ Jesus.

How is it, you may ask, that a Christian can be so controlled by these influences? Aren't we saved and bought by the blood of Christ? The answer is yes. Of course we are. But the battle we're talking about here has nothing to do with our salvation, which is a matter of spirit. The battleground is in our minds, which still lie under the influence of the world and are in the process of being transformed. From that old self, from that old mindset, we have heard and believed lies.

> *Do not lie to one another, since you laid aside the old self with its evil practices, and have put on the new self who is being renewed to a true knowledge according to the image of the One who created him* (Colossians 3:9-10).

Here Paul is telling us that there is an old "self" or mind that is being renewed or renovated so that it agrees with the salvation we have received in our spirits. This old self or mind not only reflects our old sinful and carnal nature, but it also carries with it the wounds and the memories from the past along with the lies that provide them the soil to live in. The lies that were planted in our past still bear fruit in the present.

The process that uncovers these lies and allows us an unobstructed view of God is what we refer to as inner healing. Paul, dealing with the believers in Rome, describes the process of rooting out the lies of the world as "renewing the mind."

> *And do not be conformed to this world, but be transformed by the renewing of your mind, so that you may prove what the will of God is, that which is good and acceptable and perfect* (Romans 12:2).

What is untrue has no power unless we believe it. And if we experience it enough, we may come to believe even a greater lie. Jesus said that even the very elect, those close to God, can be deceived (see Mk. 13:22). Of course, in that passage Jesus was speaking of false messiahs, but the principle is the same for any other lie. In the opening story about Carol, it was not true that she was unacceptable or unlovable, but she had heard and experienced disapproval from a respected adult teacher and came to believe it. (To be sure, she had other, similar memories, but the Lord chose that particular one to reveal His heart to Carol.) Nevertheless, what was totally false and baseless gained power over Carol's life. Until she learned the truth, her life was bound by a lie.

Everything we believe is not necessarily true. We come to believe something by our experience or perhaps through the environment in which we grew up. At the same time, God's love for us and His desire to see us healed and in fellowship with Him is true. Our believing it does not make it true—it is true so we can believe it!

The traveling companion of truth is peace. As we mentioned earlier, peace, or *shalom* in Hebrew, refers to a state of wholeness. The relationship between truth and peace is seen throughout the Scriptures. Truth brings healing, as the Lord spoke through the prophet Jeremiah in referring to His desire to restore the lost nation of Israel: "Behold, I will bring to it health and healing, and I will heal them; and I will reveal to them an abundance of peace and truth" (Jer. 33:6). *Truth brings order, and order brings peace or wholeness.*

The Healing Truth

The truest thing in the universe is that God loves us. The Scriptures say, "God is love" (1 Jn. 4:8). The truth of God's love was nailed to the cross and put on display for the world to see. His love was *real*. This was the glory of God, who made us pure by His own blood and enabled us to return to fellowship with the Father. Unfortunately, even though we are saved and reunited with God in spirit, our minds are still caught in the thorns of Eden's curse. It is because we as Christians do not understand who we are and what Christ has done for us—the truth—that we still experience fear, rejection, worthlessness, shame, powerlessness, and hopelessness. God's desire is to bring us the truth to heal our wounded and distorted emotions.

Actually, the truth that brings us healing is not merely a correction of inadequate data; the Truth is the presence and voice of Jesus Christ

Himself. Since separation from God is the source of all wounds and emotional dysfunction, our restoration to intimacy in His presence then becomes the source of our healing.

In the following chapters we will learn that Christ, the harbinger of God's love and acceptance, destroys each of the lies we believe about God and ourselves. God desires to bring us into the truth and peace within intimate fellowship with Himself. We serve a healing and restoring God who is not content to leave us in our emotional pain, but who leads us to Himself and the restoration of our fellowship with Him.

Now let me close with this prophetic pronouncement: The Lord loves you and He intends to bring you to a new place of intimacy and healing in His presence. Oh, how the Lord longs to bring you into His presence and pour out His healing grace upon you. He will become your Teacher—the voice of truth in your heart that destroys all the false images and lies that have robbed you of His abundant life. The Lord Himself will lead you as He speaks to you. Listen and turn toward His voice.

Hear now the words of the prophet Isaiah:

*But the Lord still waits for you to come to Him so He can show you His love and compassion. For the Lord is a faithful God. Blessed are those who wait for Him to help them. O people of Zion, who live in Jerusalem, you will weep no more. He will be gracious if you ask for help. He will respond instantly to the sound of your cries. Though the Lord gave you adversity for food and affliction for drink, He will still be with you to teach you. **You will see your teacher with your own eyes, and you will hear a voice say, "This is the way; turn around and walk here."** Then you will destroy all your silver idols and gold images. You will throw them out like filthy rags. "Ugh!" you will say to them. "Begone!"* (Isaiah 30:18-22 NLT)

Chapter Three

EMOTIONAL ECHOES

Man is disturbed not by things, but by what he believes about them.
— Epictetus, a Stoic philosopher of the first century

There is a sound I recall from my school days that still has the power to make me cringe today. You remember it. The teacher would be standing at the chalkboard writing and suddenly his or her fingernail would scrape against the board. The result was a kind of dry squealing sound that disrupted every nerve in our bodies from the roots of our teeth to the curled toes on our feet. What this small sound lacked in decibels it more than made up for in its ability to immobilize everybody within earshot. You may wince even now as the recollection of this sound overpowers you. What you heard and felt in that classroom long ago echoes in your mind today.

An echo is a voice or sound reflecting off some distant object. Think of being in a large canyon with a long distance across the chasm. You shout, and a few seconds later your voice hits the hard walls of the opposite side of the canyon and bounces back to you. An echo also can be a voice that agrees with or reflects another voice. For instance, we might "echo" someone's opinion. The bottom line is that echoes sound the same across distance, whether that distance is of time or space. The memory of that sound of fingernails on a chalkboard is an echo reflecting off of an experience long ago.

There are other "sounds"—echoes of the past—that have the ability to cause us to cringe in the present. These are emotional echoes or associations that control us.[4] Just like that screeching sound we remember from our school days, these "sounds" set off a response in us that causes us to recoil in fear, rejection, worthlessness, or some other strong negative

---

4. "Emotional echo" is a term coined by Edward M. Smith in *Beyond Tolerable Recovery*, page 39.

emotion. We all experience these controlling emotional echoes to one degree or another. We encounter an emotional echo when an experience today reflects off of one that felt the same in the past, then bounces back to us with the same emotion of the original event. In other words, I feel now whatever I felt then.

All of us have experienced some kind of controlling emotional echo, whether it was loud or barely audible. These echoes control us in the sense that they cause us to act in ways that the world would see as irrational or out of proportion. There may be times when the slightest provocation causes us to blow up in anger or shrink back in terror. We know when we are under these echoes' control because our emotional response is out of balance with what is happening around us. It is as if one sound is being created around us, but we hear something totally different from what everyone else does. Someone is playing a violin, and we are hearing an oboe. Remember, I am talking about Christians here—people bought by the blood of the Lamb of God and bound for glory. Whatever the cause, the resulting negative feelings seize control of us and rob us of the benefits of our life in Christ.

I remember once witnessing what seemed to be a ridiculous argument about a car. Two men had recently purchased similar cars, and one man remarked to the other that their cars were pretty much the same. The second man flew into an irrational tirade that the cars were not the same, that his car was a newer and better model than the other man's. You'd have thought that the first man had spit in the other's face. "Who cares what kind of car they had?" we might say to ourselves. This was about more than cars, you see. The enraged man stormed out the door, leaving the other man shrugging his shoulders wondering what had caused such a heated response.

Looking back now, it seemed as though the man who became angry believed he had to be right—he had to have something better. The casual comment his friend made regarding the car set in motion an echo from somewhere in his past that told him he had to be right or risk being somehow devalued as a person. The argument in the present was not about cars; it was about the man's self-worth—it was an emotional echo.

Something "greater and stronger" was controlling the man in the illustration. His response had little to do with a car. It was an echo—a tie to some other place in his life that felt like the present event. He was living in two places and two events at one time—the past and the present—and feeling the same about both. He had been threatened in the past and that emotion traveled into the present. One man was talking about cars and the other about life itself.

Feeling What We Believe

There is a relationship between what we *feel* and what we *believe*. Our emotions are not based on what is absolutely true, but what feels true to us. What we *feel* is the product of what we *believe*, and what we believe is a product of what we have *experienced*. The order is *experience, beliefs*, then *feelings*.[5]

For example, two men may be walking down the street and they encounter a big black dog, but based upon their own life experiences, they may feel entirely different about the dog. A big black dog may have bitten one of the men as a child while the other may have grown up in a family that owned a big black dog. One person will feel fear and the other joy at seeing the same big black dog under the same conditions and at the same time. Nevertheless, what they experienced previously determines what they believe. Both of them feel as they did earlier in their lives because they believe what they believed then. So, as Epictetus the Stoic said, "Man is disturbed not by things, but by what he believes about them" (paraphrased).

In the course of everyday life, our minds pick up thousands of words and thoughts. Some of them stay with us while the rest fade away—they are deleted from our memory. The things that stick with us, however, usually are associated with some strong emotions of some kind, whether pleasant or not. These past emotions are the hard surfaces off of which our present emotions echo.

Those of us who are old enough will never forget where we were when we heard that President John F. Kennedy was shot. I was at Central Junior High School walking down a flight of stairs on my way to science class with Mrs. Oliver when a kid came running up the stairs to tell us what he had seen on TV.

5. For further study on the connection of emotions and beliefs see "Renewing Mind," *Rational Christian Thinking*, by Alice Petersen, Gary Sweeten, and Dorothy Faye Geverdt, pages 3:1 through 3:21. Also see chapter three of *Beyond Tolerable Recovery* by Edward Smith, pages 39-57.

I also can remember what I had for supper the day our daughter Amy was born. I had chili in the hospital cafeteria. It was lousy, but I remember it. The feeling I had about President Kennedy's assassination was of sorrow and the emotion I experienced at my daughter's birth was joy. Both strongly resonate in my memory. I feel now what I felt then whenever those memories are triggered.

All in all, there are several distant surfaces off of which our emotions might be reflected—places where what we feel now is a reflection of what we felt then. Here are a few of them.

Distant Reflective Surfaces

Trauma, Joy

Have you ever been in a traffic accident? Perhaps there's a certain street that you used to drive down every day without any thought or remembrance. But one day while on that street, another car bumped into yours. You might, even now, still remember the time of day, what you were wearing, the name of the other driver, the color of the car that hit yours, or any number of other things. Not only that, but now each time you drive through that spot your hands might tighten a little bit on the steering wheel and you may look around a little harder because of the trauma of the accident. Why does this happen? It's all because your present thoughts and feelings are echoes from the previous trauma.

Our present emotions also can bounce off of times of repeated abuse. Each wound or event gives opportunity for a lie to be recorded in our minds that plays back when we are reminded of the original event. It can be deliberate embarrassment, physical abuse, or sexual abuse. But when someone comes along who has a similar voice, dresses the same way, or appears in a similar situation, we may begin to feel the same kind of fear or nausea we felt in those times of abuse. The trigger to this echo can be just about anything—as long as it reminds us of what happened before. (There will be several examples of these kinds of abuse in the chapters ahead.)

Family Dysfunction

Those who grow up in dysfunctional families (and most families are dysfunctional in one way or another) may hear echoing voices from parents, teachers, or others telling us that we are not good enough. I have heard adults make such statements, reflecting the past, as, "You're just stupid," or "You will never be anything . . ." Believe it or not, these things may have been recorded decades earlier and become part of the operating system of the one who heard them. Each time that person has a challenge or an opportunity, he or she hears these words bouncing off the hard wall of the distant past.

Sometimes family dysfunction may appear in the inability to show affection or love among family members. I can't tell you how many times I have heard someone say, "We just weren't a 'huggy' family...we knew that we were loved, but we didn't show it physically." Some of those whom we have heard say something like this struggle with feelings of worthlessness or insecurity today. There was a lie at work in that family that said love did not have to be demonstrated. That lie echoes today in their families, who also have trouble showing affection. Some end up with rebellious kids and have extramarital affairs.

Generational Sin

There are lies that grow on family trees as well. Today these might be referred to as generational sin. Here's a simple description of the concept of generational sin: If the parents plant poison ivy in the backyard, their children are going to itch. Parents set the tone in the family—they establish a family culture. Children naturally pick up what the parents demonstrate. Children often echo things that we don't want to hear. If Daddy treats Mommy with disdain and disrespect, then little Suzy may grow up looking for a husband to treat her the same way.

The Bible says that the sins committed in the family will come knocking on the door of subsequent generations. God told Moses and Israel not to give their children to the pagan influences and families around them. God said, "You shall not worship them or serve them; for I, the Lord your God, am a jealous God, visiting the iniquity of the fathers on the children, on the third and the fourth generations of those who hate Me" (Ex. 20:5). The "them" God was talking about are false gods and influences like fear, rejection, shame, and all the rest. Children live with the consequences of their parents' choices, not necessarily the guilt of them. In fact, they have a better-than-even chance of doing whatever it was that they saw their parents doing. If the parents serve those false gods and influences, then the children will as well.

Culture

Our feelings today—how we think of and how we relate to the world around us—may spring from the culture in which we were raised. There may be echoes of racial prejudice, gender bias, religious self-righteousness, or any manner of other such fruit growing out of a culture. For example, a young girl may grow up in a culture that tells her she is inferior and only good for having babies. She will be discouraged from going to school and developing her own abilities and talents. In another instance, one person may look down on another simply because of the individual's mode of dress or religious appearance.

I must include the Church as a source of cultural emotional echoes. I suspect there is a lot of guilt and fear in the pews of the church. The place that ought to be the fountain of grace has sometimes been the source of wounding and shame.

Sin Not Confessed

Some emotional echoes may be the result of sin that has not been dealt with. Many times we have ministered to people who have such a nagging sense of guilt or shame that they just can't move on with their lives. The problem may be that they never really confessed a sin in the past. In such cases the issue is resolved simply by confessing and then receiving grace and forgiveness in the presence of God.

Most likely there are other origins for the emotional echoes we hear in our present lives. But regardless of the source—the distant reflection point of the emotional echo—we must find a way to silence them...to delete or erase the lies upon which they resonate.

Silencing the Echoes

God's best is not for us to live under the power of the toxic tapes that play in our emotions today. God showed Moses and the nation of Israel a way to silence the negative influences that threatened to control their lives. He promised to deliver these nations and influences into our hands for us to destroy. In the next few chapters we will spend time locating the lies off of which our current emotions echo and silence them by bringing the truth of God.

The Spirit of God hears each of the emotional reflections in our hearts and is even now beginning to identify them to you. These are the places where you feel afraid, shameful, or unsafe. They are the reasons you become angry at the slightest provocation or depressed at every turn. I pray that the Lord will open the eyes of your heart to see His heart and healing that you might be released from those hurtful echoes from the past.

> *I pray that the eyes of your heart may be enlightened, so that you will know what is the hope of His calling, what are the riches of the glory of His inheritance in the saints, and what is the surpassing greatness of His power toward us who believe. These are in accordance with the working of the strength of His might which He brought about in Christ, when He raised Him from the dead and seated Him at His right hand in the heavenly places, far above all rule and authority and power and dominion, and every name that is named, not only in this age but also in the one to come. And He put all things in subjection under His feet, and gave Him as head over all things to the church, which is His body, the fullness of Him who fills all in all* (Ephesians 1:18-23).

Chapter Four

TEARING DOWN ALTARS

All of us want to find a place of greater peace and intimacy with our Creator. We all want to dwell in His presence, to hear His voice clearly. Sometimes, instead of enjoying that peace, we are bombarded by nagging thoughts and inner voices vying for our attention and robbing us of peace and intimacy with God. These thoughts and voices are the things wired into us; they're our software. We cannot help but hear those voices and feel those emotions that control us, any more than we can help breathing in and out. The folks around us don't see what we see or feel what we feel. They have their own software problems to deal with. But there is help and healing for the influences that bind and control us. Now is the time to take out the garbage that has invaded our peace.

God has given us His Word to show us how to dismantle those influences and uncover the lies that bind us, so that we can live close to Him. He told Israel in Deuteronomy 7 that He would deliver those seven nations—those influences—them and give them an opportunity to destroy those nations. Like the Israelites, we too can destroy those influences in our lives and live free. For the rest of this chapter, we will focus on uncovering the simple process by which the Lord allows us to find freedom and healing in His presence.

Instruction for Destruction

As Moses and Israel prepared to cross into the place of peace and abundance that God had prepared for them, God gave them specific instructions on how to eliminate the influences that could keep them from enjoying the peace and rest He had provided for them. These nations represented influences like *fear, rejection, worthlessness, shame, insecurity, defilement,* and *hopelessness*. The Lord gave His people instructions for the destruction of these nations and the influences they represented.

43

*But thus you shall do to them: you shall **tear down their altars,
and smash their sacred pillars**, and **hew down their Asherim**,
and **burn their graven images with fire*** (Deuteronomy 7:5).

The instructions God gave to Moses told them to…

- "Tear down their altars." Locate and dismantle the pagan influences.
- "Smash their sacred pillars." Get rid of the things that remind them of those pagan influences.
- "Hew down their Asherim." Find and uncover places of darkness where these influences live.
- "Burn their graven images with fire." Purify and get rid of the false images or lies about God and all that those images represent.

The instructions God gave to Moses for eliminating pagan influences in the Promised Land reflect, in principle, the process through which we today seek out and destroy the lies and controlling emotional influences that stem from past inner wounds—wounds that still cause us limitation today. We basically follow the same instructions: tear down, smash, hew down, and burn. Altars, pillars, Asherim, and fire represent parts of the process of emotional healing. They are as follows.

Altar—An altar represents the influences that causes us to feel controlling negative emotions today (such as fear, etc.).

Pillar—A pillar represents an emotional echo or triggering event that causes us to feel what we feel.

Asherim—Asherim represents the hidden dark place in the past where the lie was first planted.

Fire—Fire represents the truth of God that destroys the lies we have believed and have controlled us.

If we are to be free of controlling emotional influences, then we must find out *what* we feel, *when* we feel it, *why* we tend to feel or be controlled by that emotion, and what the healing *truth* is. It is a process that starts in the present, reflects the past, and leads us to the future.

The Lord instructed Moses to tear down the altars of the people that the Israelites were to displace. That is what we need to do when a strong negative emotion keeps us bound and living short of the abundance God intends for us. We need to tear down those altars.

"Tear Down Their Altars"

An altar was a place where blood or life was presented. It was a place of submission and control where the worshiper presented his or her life and hope to a deity. The gods that these seven nations worshiped were false gods. In other words, they did not exist. Rather, each one represented a false idea about the true God. They were lies that engendered fear and performance rather than the love and acceptance that are available in God.

When we tear down altars today, we are discovering and dismantling the power of the lies that control us and our emotions. As we discussed in the previous chapter, our emotions flow from what we believe. We *feel* what we *believe*, and we *live* what we *feel*. For example, if I believe the world is a dangerous place, then I feel fear or insecurity. That fear then keeps me locked up and barricaded behind the walls of my house.

Again, if we are to dismantle the lies that control us, we must first find out what is controlling us. Is it fear, rejection, or shame? We can begin to get an idea of the lies that control us by looking at how we live and what we feel. These controlling lies are on display every day. Think of the person who never went to college because he was told he was not smart enough, or the one who abused her children because she was abused. Whatever the lie, it will direct us down prescribed paths that lead us away from God.

Sometimes only one emotion seems to control us, such as the "shame" that controlled my wife Carol and kept her limited around the belief that she just couldn't do anything well enough. Remember the man in the argument about the car? His life was controlled by the lie that told him he was not safe somehow, and therefore he felt threatened any time someone disagreed with him.

The second part of this book is filled with word pictures extracted from the Bible that describe how ordinary people lived under the influence of certain lies and emotions. We will also examine each of the controlling influences mentioned in Deuteronomy 7, along with the emotional profile they create. However, for now here is a very brief summary of each of them.

Altars—The Lies That Control Us

Fear is based on the lie that we are all alone in dangerous waters. It is the first emotion mentioned in the Bible and the root of all other negative emotions. Fear makes us want to run and hide. When we are controlled by fear, we avoid life. We don't take chances or experience anything new. We tremble at the thought of what might be around the next corner.

Rejection is the lie that we don't fit in, that we don't belong. When we feel rejected, we seem to wander around in a state of anonymous confusion as to who and what we are. When rejection controls us, we sit by the wall waiting for someone to sign our dance card, all the time believing no one ever will.

Worthlessness is exactly that: the lie that we are worth less than others to whom we compare ourselves. We look at those around us and believe that we are not as good as they are. When we live under worthlessness, we spend most of our time striving to prove that we are worth the air and the space we take up. Seldom do we get to any place of self-worth.

Shame is the lie that we have crossed the line of God's grace, that we are not worthy of His love. Shame is like a toxic mud made up of failure that tells us we are not good enough. It makes us hang our heads and cover our faults like Adam and Eve, who tried to cover their nakedness with fig leaves. Shame also can apply outside the moral law of God and extend to any part of our lives where we believe we are "not good enough." Shame blocks us from intimacy with God and keeps us focused on our shortcomings.

Insecurity is the lie that says everything is a threat and no one is in control. Those under the lie of insecurity are constantly on the watch for the next wave of attacks. They live in a limping unsafety, believing they are helpless victims whose life and world are out of control. When we feel out of control, we try to find ways to take control of everything and everyone using every tool from emotional manipulation to addictions of all kinds. Shame keeps us in "Fortress Us." We trust nobody.

Defilement is the lie that tells us that it's over, that we are ruined for life. Defilement happens when an innocent victim is abused by someone he or she should have been able to trust. People who live under defilement believe that they will never be the same again. They live with a dirty feeling. They wear the guilt of the one who sinned against them and find it hard to experience intimacy of any kind.

Hopelessness is the lie that tells us we will never…whatever it is, we will never…. Those who are hopeless see the cup half empty without any way of refilling it. Hopelessness leaves us stooped over and stuck looking into blackness. When we live under the influence of hopelessness, we just quit.

All of us experience most of these emotions in the course of our lives, but when they begin to control us and interfere with all that God has for us, we need to deal with them. We need to *tear them down.*

Tearing something down means dismantling it. The altars that control us were built one wound at a time, just like an altar of stone is built one stone at a time. As a result, we have to tear them down one stone at a time. The Hebrew word translated as "tear down," *nathats*, implies that the influences that control us were built up and now must be torn down the same way, over a period of time.

We can know what influence is controlling us by what we feel. Emotions are the medium by which our minds interpret the world around us. What we feel about things, events, and people, is based on what we *believe* about them. It is not as simple as saying, "I'm afraid" or "I'm ashamed." There are a host of emotions and feelings that flow from the influence that controls us. These feelings are listed in the chapters that describe the various influences.

"Smash Their Sacred Pillars"

The pillars referred to in Deuteronomy 7:5 were a kind of memorial or image of the deity associated with the altar. It was a reminder of the lie that that deity represented. In our application, a pillar represents a trigger that reminds us of the lie we believe, which results in the emotions we feel. These triggers are like the "emotional echoes" referred to in the previous chapter. They are the *when* we feel *what* we feel.

For example, someone living under the lie of rejection may go to a family reunion and end up sitting all alone. He or she feels out of place at such a social function. Chances are that the other family members at the reunion have no idea that the person feels rejected by them. They may, in fact, say that this person does not like the family or is aloof. We need to be careful how we judge someone's heart. We are usually wrong. Perhaps when the rejected person was very young, he or she was left to be raised by a relative. Though that child may have been cared for, he or she still feels out of place. Now, anytime there is a family function, that person is reminded of the abandonment and feels rejected and out of place.

The reunion was the *pillar*—the triggering event that reminded the person of the lie that he or she doesn't belong.

We run into these triggering pillars all day long. They may be as simple as a similar name or physical appearance of a person or place. They may be a familiar smell. For example, when I smell mothballs, I think of my maternal grandmother. When my brother and I were very young, we used to go to her house, and many times we took a nap there. I'm not sure now as I write whether that was because we needed a rest or whether grandmother did. In any event, at naptime my grandmother would go to her cedar chest and pull out this gray woolen blanket with blue dots on it. We would curl up in the blanket and someone—either us or our grandmother—got to rest. The mothballs or the smell of that cedar chest is a *pillar* that releases warm and loving feelings in my memory.

There are many other pillars that evoke feelings of terror or shame. For example, a woman who has been sexually abused may feel trapped any time she is in a small room with any man. That small room triggers feelings of fear because it reminds her of a place where she was abused. Whatever the pillar, it is a reminder of a lie or a belief that controls our lives.

We are instructed to smash these sacred pillars. The Hebrew word translated as "smash" here is *shabar*, which means to crush or to break into pieces. When we smash these pillars, we are breaking their ability to control and divert us. How do we smash these reminders of pain? We have to look to the times in our present-day lives when we tend to feel the strong emotions that take control of us. Maybe I feel fear when I enter a crowded room, or maybe I feel ashamed any time my spouse and I discuss intimacy. Remember, when we talk about tearing down altars, we are finding *what* we feel that stems from a lie we believe. When we smash pillars, we are determining *when* we feel that way.

When do we feel rejected? *When* do we feel shameful? *When* do we feel hopeless and depressed? These times are the sacred pillars, which are more like those brightly colored plastic cones that restrict us in construction areas. When we know what we feel and when we feel it, we can begin to trace them to a source.

"Hew Down Their Asherim"

The King James Version translates Asherim as "groves," which is a good picture of what they really were. These were groves of trees— places where light was blotted out and truth obscured. They were places of secret sinning in Canaanite religion. For our purpose, the Asherim is the place of darkness in the past *where* a wound occurred and a lie was enabled.

The limiting lies we believe in the present, as well as the emotions that accompany them, are rooted somewhere in the past. It is not always obvious why we believe or feel what we do. Sometimes lies are rooted in sudden traumatic events; sometimes they are part of the environment in which we were raised. Either way, the Asherim are the distant reflective surfaces off of which emotional echoes bounce.

When we are "hewing down Asherim," we are going to the place of darkness by asking the Lord, in prayer, to bring us a memory picture of where the lie and the controlling emotions are rooted. We want to find the place *where* we began to feel what we feel and so uncover the lies we believe. The use of the word *hew* implies going to a place where something living was planted and is still shooting its obscuring foliage into our present, obstructing our vision of God and the abundant life He intends for us. When we find this place, we cut it down like a tree that hangs over our house, threatening to crash through the roof.

Sometimes more than one memory will surface where the lie is expressed. In that case we try to find the oldest memory in which the lie was rooted. However, sometimes a lie is so much a part of our culture or past that we cannot locate the very first time we began to believe that lie and take on the emotions associated with it. It is not as important to find the oldest memory as much as it is to find the place where the false beliefs and emotions are clearly represented. In that case, when the lie is uncovered, it is uncovered everywhere and anywhere it was alive. What we are looking for when we hew down Asherim is a place where we can uncover the source of the lie and bring truth to it, which brings us to the last part of the process God outlined for us to destroy the limiting lies that bind us.

"Burn Their Graven Images with Fire"

The ultimate method of purifying anything is through *fire*. Fire can remove anything that is not pure or true. When we want to remove impurities from gold, we subject it to fire to melt it down. The heat and the fire separate what is gold (what is eternal) from what is dross (imperfections, things that are not gold). In the same way, we submit the lies we believe to the fire of God's truth to separate them and allow truth to emerge. Anything that can be burned is not eternal, or of God.

There is fire all through the Old Testament, especially in the Torah. It was fire that purified Sodom and Gomorrah (see Gen. 19:24). God revealed Himself to Moses in a burning bush (see Ex. 3:2). It was fire that led the Israelites' way in the wilderness (see Ex. 14:24). It was fire that accompanied the presence of God on Mount Sinai (see Ex. 19:18). It is fire that consumes flesh, the carnality of the sacrifice (see Ex. 29:18).

Fire represents the holiness and purity of God, and most especially the truth of His Word. We hear His Word from the midst of the fire (see Deut. 4:36). It is the truth of God's Word that incinerates and separates the lies from the truth.

After we find out *what* lies control us, *when* they control us, and *where* they were planted, we submit those lies to the *truth* of God. In fact, we submit them to the truth of God as expressed in His manifested presence in the memory picture. Quoting Scripture is great, but the presence of God in the truth is what incinerates the lies. The Bible says, "The Lord reigns, let the earth rejoice; let the many islands be glad. Clouds and thick darkness surround Him; righteousness and justice are the foundation of His throne. Fire goes before Him and burns up His adversaries round about" (Ps. 97:1-3). Those "adversaries" or enemies are the things that keep us away from God. They are *fear, rejection, worthlessness, shame, insecurity, defilement,* and *hopelessness*—the "ites" that inhabit the promise of abundant life in the presence of God.

Once the Lord has taken us to a root memory where the lie is contained, we simply ask Him to reveal to us His presence and the truth regarding the situation in the memory picture. It is the fiery presence of the truth of God that incinerates and destroys the presence of the lie. No lie can withstand the presence of God.

> But who can endure the day of His coming? And who can stand when He appears? For He is like a refiner's fire and like fullers' soap (Malachi 3:2).

The Sound of Truth

We might ask how we can know whether God is the one speaking to us, or if it is our own human thoughts, or even if it is the enemy. The best way to discern what we are hearing is to keep in mind this simple fact:

The truth of God reflects the character of God. We can know something is the truth of God's Word to us by the character and effect of it. Psalm 19:7-10 gives us a good idea of the character of God's truth. In this psalm there are several synonyms for the communication of God: the law, testimony, precepts, commandment, fear, or the judgments of God. We can listen to what we hear and compare it to the sound of truth in this psalm.

> *The law of the Lord is perfect, **restoring the soul**; the testimony of the Lord is sure, **making wise the simple**. The precepts of the Lord are right, **rejoicing the heart**; the commandment of the Lord is pure, **enlightening the eyes**. The fear of the Lord is clean, **enduring forever**; the judgments of the Lord are true; they are **righteous altogether**. They are **more desirable than gold**, yes, than much fine gold; sweeter also than honey and the drippings of the honeycomb* (Psalm 19:7-10).

- *The truth of God restores.* As we submit what we hear from the Lord to the Scriptures, we can easily see what is true. When God reveals truth, it restores the soul, mind, will, and emotions. It brings us back to the truth; it's as if it reboots our system with the original settings. If we are hearing the thoughts of and experiencing the presence of God, we will be restored—literally turned in a new direction toward God and away from the lies and all they convey.

- *The truth brings wisdom; it enlightens the eyes.* Wisdom is the putting together of truth. It is not enough to have the facts. Truth leads us toward a change in our view of God. We see things literally in a new light—the light of His presence—not according to the wounds and lies that have controlled us. "In Your light we see light" (Ps. 36:9b). It brings about a change in the way we see life and even how we view those who have wounded us.

- *The truth rejoices the heart.* Truth brings joy. In the presence of the Lord there is fullness of joy (see Ps. 16:11). We are removed from a life held under the circumstances and are no longer bound by wounds. We are beyond happy; we are removed to a place in God that is beyond the balance in our checkbooks. God does not speak to us to scold us and push us away; rather, He invites us to healing and Himself.

- *The truth is as eternal as gold.* God does not speak to us about old scars and new scars. God reveals the eternal to us. What God says was true in the past, is true now and will be true as God's promise in the future.

- *The truth of God carries with it the sweetness of God.* Above all other things, the truth of God brings with it the sense of His sweetness. God's character flows out of His love and compassion. When Moses asked God to show him His glory—what He was all about—God displayed His character in front of him.

Then the Lord passed by in front of him and proclaimed, "The Lord, the Lord God, compassionate and gracious, slow to anger, and abounding in lovingkindness and truth" (Exodus 34:6).

When we hear the truth of God, it will reflect the character of God and bring us to the awareness of the presence of God. In His presence there is healing from all the lies and wounds that bind us. We are free to live in His presence and to enjoy rest and peace, communion and shared purpose.

The Voice of Truth

God reveals His truth to us in an unlimited number of ways; we need to pay attention and listen carefully to hear Him. Whatever way God chooses to speak, it is always clear and unambiguous to the listener. God is not out to trick us. Why would God lead us to healing, then make His truth so complicated that we don't get it? God wants to speak to us, and He will do so in a way that is clear and life-bringing.

Also, do not limit what the Lord says or how He says it. We have heard the Lord speak in words of Scripture, through sensations such as warmth or light, and sometimes by just the feeling of a surrounding presence. Sometimes the Lord has brought other memories to us that contain the truth He is speaking to us. I have ministered to some who saw the faces of other people who represented what the Lord was saying. The key to hearing the truth that God is speaking in a memory picture is to listen and just receive it, not try to figure out what He will say. It is not a cognitive process as much as a spiritual experience. You might say that *if we are going to hear God, we need to be out of our minds.* God may not say what we *think* He will say, but He will always say what we *need* Him to say.

Hearing the voice of God is not the province of a privileged and especially holy few. It is the right of all children of God in Christ who are led of the Spirit. God has longed to speak to us and heal us. We must listen with an open and rested heart, expecting God to bring the fire to burn up the lies that have kept us bound. *He will do it!*

Clean the House and Close the Door

Jesus also instructed His disciples in some house-cleaning details after deliverance.

> *Now when the unclean spirit goes out of a man, it passes through waterless places seeking rest, and does not find it. Then it says, "I will return to my house from which I came"; and when it comes, it finds it unoccupied, swept, and put in order. Then it goes and takes along with it seven other spirits more wicked than itself, and they go in and live there; and the last state of that man becomes worse than the first. That is the way it will also be with this evil generation* (Matthew 12:43-45).

When we have received truth we must "sweep the house," attending to the following details.

- If the lie was embedded because of sin, we must confess the sin along with any soul ties that resulted from any sexual sins.

- If the lie was the result of family lies, we must renounce and break any generational sin/lies and confess the truth.

- If the lie was the result of an offense or abuse by other people, we must forgive them by stating what they did, how we felt about it, and the lie we believed; then we forgive and release them in the name of Jesus Christ.

- We must address any unclean spirit that may have attached itself to the lie. Command it to leave in the name of Jesus Christ.

When we have done all these things, the enemy and the lies he speaks have no place to run and no place to hide. We do not have to spend a lot of time shouting at demons. Demons cannot survive in the presence of Truth, which is in fact the presence of God. When the Truth shows up, the enemy must flee.

When I was in my late twenties, I lived in a nice apartment outside Latrobe, Pennsylvania. The only downfall about the apartment was the field across from it in which people had dumped old furniture and junk. All that trash brought the presence of rats, which occasionally scurried across the parking lot. It was unsettling, to say the least.

One day the landlord brought in a backhoe and hauled out several truckloads of trash. When the trash was removed, there were no more rats. Demons are the rats, and the lies are the trash that litters our lives. If you will get rid of the trash, or the lies, then the rats, the demons, will go away.[6]

When we have heard the truth and have taken out the trash, we need to go back to the current triggering event and apply the same truth to it. When we look at that recent pillar or triggering event, whatever was true in the past is now true there as well. The peace we found in the past now fills the present and becomes a promise from God into the future.

What follows is a very abbreviated version of a typical ministry session, so that you can see it broken into its various components. This sample is not all you need to know to facilitate ministry to other people, but rather a picture of the flow of the ministry as we have experienced it. Once again, I suggest that you seek training from others who are competent and experienced in inner healing before you attempt to facilitate this ministry.

Sample Ministry Session

Lester was a man in his late fifties who was referred to us by a friend. He was an affable man with a southern charm and wit. I had seen him many times over the years, and his most pronounced feature was his warm smile. However, Lester was not smiling this day. All his smiles had given way to a sober seriousness.

We opened the time together by welcoming the presence of the risen and exalted Christ, remembering His promise that "where two or three have gathered together in My name, I am there in their midst" (Mt. 18:20).

---

6.   I was reminded of my own personal experiences with rats as I read *Deep Wounds, Deep Healing* by Charles Kraft, page 258.

Altar

Lester was feeling hopeless and rejected. As we walked through the emotional profile, feelings of rejection were verified.

Pillar

We discussed what Lester was feeling, and I asked about a recent time when he experienced those feelings. He related the scene of his wife's leaving him without explanation. He recounted how she said she was going to work, but then called him to tell him she was not coming home again. Lester was shocked and felt utterly rejected. He rehearsed over and over again the many times he had been rejected.

As Lester recalled the present experience, I asked him, "What do you feel as you look at this recent memory picture?"

Lester replied, "I feel alone—I will always be alone."

Asherim

With his feelings clarified, we prayed, "Lord, take Lester by the hand and lead him to the source of these feelings and beliefs he is experiencing today." With that, the Lord brought Lester to a memory of growing up in a very large family where he was one of ten children. He was kind of lost in the shuffle. The memory picture was one of Lester being taken out of his family and asked to live with an older couple who needed help. Lester moved in with them and was separated from his family. He would come home regularly, but he felt increasingly out of place—disconnected—like he no longer belonged.

When Lester finished describing the memory picture, I once again asked him, "Lester, what do you feel as you look at this picture?" Lester quickly replied as he did in the recent event with his wife: "I feel alone— I'll always be alone—I don't belong anywhere."

Fire

With that we asked the Lord to reveal His presence and truth to Lester. In a few seconds Lester was aware of the presence of God in the form of words that were repeated over and over: "You belong to Me— You belong to Me. I have always been with you, and I will always be with you." Then Lester could sense the presence of the Lord in what could only be described as a warmth that felt like, "It's okay. It will be okay."

For a long time Lester had believed that somehow he was alone and that perhaps there was something unacceptable about him since his parents sent him away and his wife left him. But the truth was that he was warm in the presence of God and that God had a purpose for Lester in his living with that older couple. After this simple truth, there was a torrent of truth that flooded his mind out of his memories. The Lord began to remind Lester that because he was not with his family, he did not get into alcohol like his siblings had. In fact, the older couple whom he went to live with encouraged him to pursue things that his parents told him he could never do. God had a purpose in Lester. Lester was accepted and blessed in the presence of Christ that had always been with him.

Cleaning the House

After the flood of truth subsided, we asked Lester to think about that scene where his wife called him telling him that she was not coming home. Lester was able to forgive his wife and release her to the grace of God. As Lester recalled that recent time, he still felt sad at her leaving, but he was aware of the presence of God saying, "It's okay, Lester. I'm here."

Note to the Reader

As you move through the chapters in Part II, you will have an opportunity to understand the nature and the emotional profiles of the lies that people live under. Then you will have an opportunity to go through the same process that Lester did in the presence of Christ, comparing your life to those of others in the Bible who felt just like you do. They were regular people who got hurt, had fears, felt rejected, and all the rest. You will be asked to compare your life to theirs and journal the things that seem the same to you. Then you will be taken by the hand by the Lord Jesus Himself and brought to the source of those memories for healing. The Lord will speak the truth to you, and you will be healed!

I pray right now for an awareness in your heart of God's intention to heal you. He longs to tell you that you are loved and accepted. Allow Him to take you by the hand and lead you to healing in His presence.

Chapter Five

LOOKING BOTH WAYS

O Lord, You have searched me and known me. You know when I sit down and when I rise up; You understand my thought from afar. You scrutinize my path and my lying down, and are intimately acquainted with all my ways. Even before there is a word on my tongue, behold, O Lord, You know it all. You have enclosed me behind and before, and laid Your hand upon me. Such knowledge is too wonderful for me; it is too high, I cannot attain to it (Psalm 139:1-6).

Back when our children were very small, I would never have dreamed of allowing them to cross the street by themselves. There is a lot of traffic on Main Street, even in our quiet little town. When we would come to the corner, we'd wait for the light to change so that we could safely cross. When the light changed, we just didn't set out across the street, though; we would look to the right and to the left to make sure that it was safe. What made it safe for my children was that they did not have to cross the street alone. Their little hands were in the hand of their father. Daddy was bigger and could see farther in both directions. It was safe to cross the street with their hands in Daddy's hand.

When we begin the inner-healing process, we are crossing over from lies to truth, from wounds to healing. In this crossing, we have a Father who takes our little, powerless hand into His strong hand and He looks both ways before we cross. The Father looks to the left, our past, and then to the right, our future, and in the safety of His grip, the present, we cross over to healing. Because our heavenly Father is bigger than we are, He can see infinitely in both directions and knows exactly where He's going. Nothing takes Him by surprise. We can trust His grip on our hand—we can feel it as we cross over. Father will not leave us alone as we find healing.

Psalm 139 is a message to those who have placed their hands in the big hands of the Father to lead them over to healing and wholeness.

God's Knowing Hands

The original Hebrew word translated as "know" in verses 1 and 2 of Psalm 139 suggests the image of a hand that has covered and discovered us. The Hebrew word *yad* also is contained in the words for power, authority, knowledge, provision, or a hand that forms or shapes us like clay. God's hand—His power, His knowledge of us, His provision for us—encompasses our lives. Everything we are and everything we have experienced is in the hand of God, including past wounds. In the ecstasy of this reality, the Psalmist begins with a word of praise: "O Lord." *Lord* is the personal name of God, *Yahweh*. This is the name by which Abraham referred to God. It is the name for the One who speaks with us in a personal, face-to-face way. The Psalmist is saying something like this: "O Lord, I praise You because You have my life in Your hands…."

The psalm tells us that God knows us intimately. Even as I write these words and you read them, God is aware of our most intimate thoughts and concerns. He can see the reasons you had for picking up this book in the first place. His hand reaches into our inner recesses to the extent that there is nothing that He is not aware of. His hand has covered every inch of us inside and out whether we are aware of it or not. God's knowing hand is like an x-ray that we cannot see, but that looks into the deepest parts of us to find injury and brokenness. Such is the intimate searching of God.

If we are honest, most times we are not aware of God's knowing and loving hand around us. God's presence surrounds and fills everything at every time whether we are aware of Him or not. When Jacob, the son of Isaac, fled from Esau, he traveled through the wilderness alone—or so he thought. Then he was awakened in the middle of the night with a vision of a ladder that went from Heaven to earth with angels ascending and descending. He was living in the presence of God and didn't know it, as the Bible says: "Surely the Lord is in this place, and I did not know it" (Gen. 28:16b). Just because Jacob was not aware of God's presence didn't change the reality that He was there.

We also live in the interactive presence of God, whether we realize it or not. The room you are in right now as you read these words is filled with radio waves and TV broadcasts; you just can't see them or hear them because you don't have a suitable receiver. But they are there, nonetheless. So is God.

Not only does God know us intimately, but He also knows every aspect of our lives. He knows when we sit down, when we get up, and all the rest. God is not removed from any part of our lives or what concerns us, nor even from what we think. As we said in an earlier chapter, what we feel is a product of what we believe, and what we believe or think is a product of our experience. Some of those experiences were good, and some of them were not so good. Some of them were places of wounding, misunderstanding, or abuse. Regardless, they are not news to God. He sees them even now and longs to pour out His healing oil upon them.

Between God's Hands

The most comforting image in Psalm 139 is that God has enclosed us behind and before and that His hand is upon us. In other words, God looks both ways in our lives. The image is of our lives being between the hands of God with His hands cupped over us, guarding us gently as we would shield a flickering candle flame from the wind. God's left hand is facing His right hand, and we are in the middle. We are totally enclosed and protected between His hands. God holds the past, future, and present firmly and tenderly in the grip of His hand as we cross the street.

For those of us stuck in this veil of tears—in the human dimension—we must bend our minds around the concept that God is not a dimensional being. God is not bound by time or space in any way. He exists outside them—He invented them—He is *Lord* of them. God is present everywhere and all the time at every instant. The Bible gives us a fuller idea of God's omnipresent perspective.

For a thousand years in Your sight are like yesterday when it passes by, or as a watch in the night (Psalm 90:4).

But do not let this one fact escape your notice, beloved, that with the Lord one day is like a thousand years, and a thousand years like one day (2 Peter 3:8).

...I am God, and there is no other; I am God, and there is no one like Me, declaring the end from the beginning, and from ancient times things which have not been done... (Isaiah 46:9-10).

It is important to know that God is, in effect, still alive in the past to bring us healing in the present. Because time or space does not limit God,

He exists in the past, future, and present all at the same time. The reality is that *God is still alive in the past to bring us healing.* He can look to the left and see when we were abused or when we began to believe things about ourselves or God, and then deliver truth and healing. God was there, and He is still there in that place when someone wounded us whether or not we were aware of Him. And what is more, God can see the future from the past. Whatever God speaks to us as truth in that past wounding is still true as a *promise in the future.* If I was not alone in the past, I will never be alone in the future.

The God Who Is Here and There

The Psalmist asks a question: "Where can I go from Your Spirit? Or where can I flee from Your presence?" (Ps. 139:7)

The simple answer is, there is nowhere we can go away from God's presence—not even the past.

> *If I ascend to heaven,* **You are there***; if I make my bed in Sheol, behold,* **You are there***. If I take the wings of the dawn, if I dwell in the remotest part of the sea,* **even there Your hand will lead me***, and Your right hand will lay hold of me. If I say, "Surely the darkness will overwhelm me, and the light around me will be night," even the darkness is not dark to You, and the night is as bright as the day. Darkness and light are alike to You* (Psalm 139:8-12).

Even when we are in total darkness of remembered abuse—when we could not sense the presence of God—God was and is with us. God is not going to let go of our hands even in remembered times of abuse. To be sure, it's hard to reconcile how the presence of God would be in that place of great abuse. But He was there.

The most common and logical question asked by abused people is, "If God was really there, why did He allow me to be abused? Why didn't He stop it?" To answer this question we have to consider again that God does not exist in nor is He limited to time and space as we understand them. God did not want that abuse to happen. Nor did He specifically allow us to be abused or wounded. Someone else chose to hurt us, and God does not override free will. If we want to sin, God will allow it, but He does not want it. God could have stopped Eve from taking that first hite, but He did not. She took it, and as a result she was separated from the presence of God.

What is true is that even in those days of great abuse and wounding, God saw a day of healing. He saw you reading these words right now. God is both here in the present with us and there in the past simultaneously. The presence of the Lord fills the past memories of abuse. As we remember those times, He is there ahead of us—waiting to bring truth and healing to our hearts.

It is important to understand that God's right hand, His hand of power, is leading us to healing. As we begin the process of inner healing, allowing God's hand to search us, He will remind us of times of wounding. These memories, these pictures, will not be pleasant to look at. Some will cause fear and put us back in touch with the source of pain in our lives. Thankfully, God is the one bringing these painful memory pictures to us in order to bring truth and to heal the wounds they contain. God is not stirring up pain to punish us, but to extinguish it.

We cannot change history. The things that happened to us are real and painful. When we are wounded physically, it is an open wound and is painful. As healing comes, the wound closes and a scar remains. The scar is a reminder of the pain, but there is no longer any pain from the wound because the wound is healed.

At this point the healed wounds of the past become tools in the hands of God for healing in other lives. They make us sensitive to others who have been wounded like us. As a result, we are able to "comfort those who are in any affliction with the comfort with which we ourselves are comforted by God" (2 Cor. 1:4). God does not waste anything. The wounds that we may think disqualify us in fact become our qualification—our redemptive résumé. Who could better understand someone who has been wounded than one who has been wounded the same way? Many of the individuals who have come through our ministry later become involved in bringing healing to others. It is a God thing and proof of healing.

At the end of Psalm 139, the Psalmist invites God to search him again:

Search me, O God, and know my heart; try me and know my anxious thoughts; and see if there be any hurtful way in me, and lead me in the everlasting way (Psalm 139:23-24).

For the remainder of this book we will be inviting God to search us, to find those areas of wounded weakness, to find thoughts that are not God's thoughts and root out any influence that robs us of intimacy with God. We will examine the various influences we live under, the altars to which our lives have been presented. We'll look at "pictures" of people in the Bible who struggled with the same things we do and who were wounded the same ways we have been. Into those pictures we'll see the presence of God flow in the fullness of grace and truth. And whatever was true for those saints is also true for us.

At the end of each chapter you will be invited to compare your life and emotions with those of the people in the Bible. Then you can ask God to bring to mind those places where anxious thoughts and wounds were implanted in your life. Allow the Lord to bring them to you. Don't work at remembering; just relax and receive the memory picture from God. Where God takes you, God intends to heal you. He will not let go of your hand.

Before you begin this process—before you read each of the following chapters—bathe yourself in the presence of God in prayer. Then, read the chapters, acknowledging God's love and desire for your healing and intimacy with Him. It is the presence of God that brings truth, order, and peace to your wounded emotions. Again, we suggest that those who have serious controlling emotional issues seek out additional help from those trained in the ministry of inner healing. Read each of the following chapters with an open spirit acknowledging the presence of God.

Those who have read this material or have participated in ministry sessions have commented that it was the emphasis on and the careful walking in the presence of God that made the difference for them. They experienced powerful healing and deliverance, and they also experienced the gentleness of His compassion and love.

Note that the Hebrew words for compassion and womb are related words.[7] When God described Himself in Exodus 34:6, He listed compassion first: *"Then the Lord passed by in front of him and proclaimed, 'The Lord, the Lord God, compassionate and gracious, slow to anger, and abounding in lovingkindness and truth.'"*

---

7.   Strongs O.T. reference number 7358 and 7356. See also the Greek word for compassion, Strongs N.T.: 4697, *splagchnizomai* (splangkh-nid'-zom-ahee); middle voice from N.T.: 4698; to have the bowels yearn, i.e. (figuratively) feel sympathy, to pity.

We are, in effect, in the womb of His love as He pours out His compassion upon us, bringing us to Himself and healing, just as it was the overflowing compassion in the heart of Jesus that preceded His healing virtue (see Mt. 20:34; Mk. 1:41). Take time inviting the presence of God as you prayerfully read the following chapters. Allow the Lord Himself to carry you through to deliverance as a mother would carry the child that is formed in her womb.

Look Both Ways

As you work through the next chapters, remember that God looks both ways. He knows what has happened in your past, what is happening now, and what will happen in your future. Whatever the Lord speaks to you in the past is true today and will be His promise to you in the future. Take it and the additional Scriptures each chapter presents as God's promises. Let them become praise in your mouth as you find healing in the presence of God.

> *Remember this, and be assured; recall it to mind, you transgressors. Remember the former things long past, for I am God, and there is no other; I am God, and there is no one like Me, declaring the end from the beginning, and from ancient times things which have not been done, saying, "My purpose will be established, and I will accomplish all My good pleasure"* (Isaiah 46:8-10).

Let's agree with David and say, "O God, You have searched me, and You know me. Keep on searching me and knowing me. I will know You better as Your hand holds my hand, directing and healing me. In all times and in all places, Lord, don't let me go."

Part II

THE PROCESS OF HEALING
WOUNDED EMOTIONS

Chapter Six

Are You Afraid of the Dark?

Fear

*Now Ahab told Jezebel all that Elijah had done, and how he
had killed all the prophets with the sword. Then Jezebel sent a
messenger to Elijah, saying, "So may the gods do to me and
even more, if I do not make your life as the life of one of them
by tomorrow about this time." And he was afraid and arose and
ran for his life and came to Beersheba, which belongs to Judah,
and left his servant there. But he himself went a day's journey
into the wilderness, and came and sat down under a juniper
tree; and he requested for himself that he might die, and said,
"It is enough; now, O Lord, take my life, for I am not better
than my fathers." He lay down and slept under a juniper tree;
and behold, there was an angel touching him, and he said to
him, "Arise, eat." Then he looked and behold, there was at his
head a bread cake baked on hot stones, and a jar of water. So
he ate and drank and lay down again. The angel of the Lord
came again a second time and touched him and said, "Arise,
eat, because the journey is too great for you." So he arose and
ate and drank, and went in the strength of that food forty days
and forty nights to Horeb, the mountain of God. Then he came
there to a cave and lodged there; and behold, the word of the
Lord came to him, and He said to him, "What are you doing
here, Elijah?" He said, "I have been very zealous for the Lord,
the God of hosts; for the sons of Israel have forsaken Your
covenant, torn down Your altars and killed Your prophets with
the sword. And I alone am left; and they seek my life, to take it
away" (1 Kings 19:1-10).*

The Portrait of Fear

It was cold and dark. The searing heat of the desert through which he had run all day had given way to an unforgiving cold that penetrated to the very core of the man lying in the darkness. He had run as far as his legs and the light could carry him. Just as his strength was running out, he spotted a small tree—a bush, really. Taking his last labored steps, he carried himself to the tree and collapsed at its roots. In his exhaustion he gasped out a labored and breathless request: "Lord, let me die."

As he lay there, his mind was filled with the scenes of the previous days. He was the one who had stood upon Mount Carmel defying hundreds of priests of Baal—taunting them in their futile cries to a nonexistent god. He was the one who had called down the fire of God's presence to consume the well-watered carcass of his offering. The blood was scarcely dry on his sword, with which he had slain those hundreds of false priests fattened at Jezebel's table. It was him! *Him!*

And now, with one little word, a harlot queen breathed a threat to him as false as the gods she served. And all he could see was fear—*terror*. He ran and ran—and ran right out of his country and into the wilderness of Judah beyond her grasp and into the lap of Yahweh. Now his tortured mind and body were trembling at the prospect of royal revenge as he muttered, "Please, Lord, let me die."

Suddenly his shallow sleep was disrupted by the jostling of someone telling him, "Wake up, wake up." As he awoke he could smell bread baking on hot stones. Opening his eyes, he saw a jar of water that had been placed next to him. There beside him was all that he would need to survive in this place of self-imposed exile.

The one who had awakened him stayed with him. "Eat up; you need your strength for the journey," he said. As Elijah felt strength returning to his body, he set out on a journey of several days to Mount Horeb, the mountain of God, the place of God's heart. Elijah climbed the desert slope and came to a cave where he sat down again in the darkness. As he sat, the word of the Lord came to him, saying, "What's the matter, Elijah?"

Elijah replied, "Lord, I've done the best I can do, and it's not enough. Now they want to kill me. Nobody understands. *I am alone.*"

The Influence of Fear

Fear seems to throw itself in front of us at every turn, making us want to run away and hide under the bed in solitude. The lie that inspires fear is that we *are alone*. What a difference it would make to be able to see the presence of God amidst our fearful circumstances.

Fear is an emotion that has the capability of shattering us, freezing us in our tracks, or melting us into ineffective paralysis. Fear is stationed like a sentinel at the frontier of all new things that we could do or experience in God. It was fear that caused an entire nation to shrink back from the abundant life in God's land of promise in Numbers 13–14. Fear always seems to pop up any time something new or unfamiliar is going to happen. We refer to it as "fear of the unknown," but in reality it is likely fear that God will not be there with us in that new place.

The first nation mentioned in Deuteronomy 7 as one that the Lord would deliver before Israel was the Hittites. The word *Hittite* springs from the Hebrew word *chatath*, which is one of the words for fear. This is fear in the sense of being broken or shattered by impending terror; it literally means "to tremble." The Hittites were a fearsome and warlike people known for their brutality to those they conquered. *Chatath* is frequently translated as "dismayed" or "discouraged" and is used in synonymous parallelism with the word fear.

Fear is the oldest and first emotion mentioned in the Bible. Adam told God, "I heard the sound of You in the garden, and I was afraid because I was naked..." (Gen. 3:10). Adam was afraid because, for the first time since his creation, he faced the world alone and in his own power. He also was afraid of the consequences of his sin. His fear was the result of his separation from God. Fear is the strongest of all the emotions we experience. I believe that God listed fear as the first influence we encounter because it is the strongest negative influence and keeps us separated from God and His purpose for us.

Fear entered the world after man sinned against God, shattering the peaceful communion he enjoyed with God. Man saw that he was "naked"—on his own and apart from God—and hid at the prospect of this separation. It is the very root and origin of all the other emotions we will talk about in this book: rejection, worthlessness, shame, insecurity, defilement, and hopelessness.

Emotional Profile of Fear

Fear creates its own unique emotional profile in us. When we live under the trembling influence of fear we feel...

Afraid

It seems obvious or redundant to say that if we live under fear, we feel afraid. But it's not as obvious as we think. To be afraid is to be filled with and controlled utterly by fear. More than any other emotion, fear has the ability to dictate how we will live. If unchecked, fear will tell us everything from how to think to how to dress. Fear will keep us locked in our homes or make us run into the desert.

To be afraid is to live with a sense of constant dread waiting for the other shoe to fall, the next killer bacteria to hit, or the bad news that might come from the mail carrier. Fear is a kind of septic hydraulic fluid that fills us and turns us involuntarily whatsoever way it desires. To be afraid means that we focus on our nakedness and not on anything else, including God. Fear involves the expectation of punishment (see 1 Jn. 4:18). When I am afraid, I live to avoid consequences rather than to love and please God.

Alone

Are you afraid of the dark? I think that all of us at some time or another were or are afraid of the dark—or are we?

When our children woke up in the middle of the night from a bad dream or at the crack of a thunderstorm, they would cry out. I don't recall ever hearing any of my children crying out, "It's dark! It's dark!" More often than not they would cry out, "Mommy, Mommy," or "Daddy, Daddy." It was not just an absence of light in their bedrooms that made them afraid; it was being alone in the dark that was the source of fear. We are not afraid of the dark; we are afraid of being alone in the dark!

The greatest fear that we experience is not against some dire circumstance or threat; it is our fear of being alone. I recall a young man whom I'll call Jacob who came to us for ministry. Jacob had grown up in the Church and seemed to be a cheerful and talented person, secure in all that he did. But there was another Jacob that few people knew.

When Jacob came to us for ministry, he seemed very unsettled. He came into the office looking around at everything as if searching for something. His face held a kind of nervous smile, but he was clearly not at ease. As we talked, it became evident that Jacob lived his life wrapped in incredible fear. Jacob was unable to sit still and was bound by an astounding array of compulsive behaviors. And though he was a large man, Jacob felt threatened by almost everything and was never able to rest.

During our prayer ministry, the Lord led Jacob to a memory of hiding under his bed in the dark where he felt safe. These times of hiding usually followed some kind of perceived threat or upset. Many times they followed frightful apocalyptic sermons about the rapture. He seemed to be afraid of everything, including God. From childhood, Jacob heard sermons about an angry and vengeful God who was distant and difficult to please, a God of religious practice and unreachable standards of perfection. Relationship with this disinterested God seemed veiled behind insurmountable demands. Jacob was sure that he was going to be left after the rapture all *alone.*

As we prayed and asked God to reveal the truth about Jacob's fear, the Lord gave Jacob a picture of Jesus crawling under that bed to be with him and saying, "You are not alone. I was with you under the bed and I will never leave you." Jacob experienced the truth of God's love as the presence of Jesus wrapped around him like a warm blanket in the darkness under his bed. The truth broke the power of the lie, and now he is no longer alone and afraid in the dark.

Nervous, Paralyzed

Fear has the ability to rivet our attention and paralyze us just as it did Elijah, keeping him in the desert in fear. Fear has done its work in me personally many times, but perhaps never more than at my very first trumpet recital in college.

When I was a freshman music major at Saint Vincent College, I was asked to play in a student recital in my first semester. This was a rare and obvious privilege because freshmen seldom or never played in any solo or student recital. That was reserved for upperclassmen. But my teacher wanted me to play a particularly difficult piece, and I agreed.

All was well with me; I had the piece down cold. I showed up at the recital wearing my best duds with my trumpet polished bright enough to blind even the most cynical stuffed shirt in the audience. I watched as the other students took the stage and created a silent running commentary in my head as to how each one fared and how thrilled the audience would be at my flawless performance. Then it was my turn.

The stage was set for my debut into collegiate musical history. They raised the lid of the grand piano so that it could accompany the brilliant spectacle that was my sound. With everything set, I strode out past the curtain and took center stage. The lights were bright in the recital hall, but I could still see that the hall was packed (Not just for me, mind you, though I'm sure I thought so at the time.) As I looked out into the darkened sea of unfamiliar faces, my heart began to beat a little faster—then faster—then faster.

Suddenly I was filled with fear. My fingers couldn't find the valve buttons on my trumpet. My trumpet, which just minutes ago had seemed like a natural extension of my body in the warm-up room, now seemed like a foreign object in my hands. It felt as though I was having one of those dreams where we are naked in front of people. What was this thing—how do you play it—what's the first note?!

The piano began the first strains of introduction, and then it was time to attack the first note, but there was no spit in my mouth. The first note came, and I pressed the trumpet so hard to my mouth I thought my front teeth were loosened. Then it came. Sounds such as I had never heard began to plop from the end of my trumpet. It sounded as if someone had stuffed something in the end of my trumpet. My mouth felt like a cotton ball. I would have given a hundred dollars for some spit in my mouth, but there was none. It was a disaster of career-ending proportions.

After about ten minutes of cackling and hooting through my now ridiculously shiny instrument, the piece was mercifully over. I was so afraid that I forgot a repeat and totally missed a whole section of music. I was terrible—frozen—paralyzed. In short, I stunk! The applause was brief and polite. I was humiliated and felt like saying, "Excuse me" on the way to find the nearest trash bin in which I might deposit my stupid trumpet. I hurried off the stage and away from my professor. Thank God, it was not my last recital, though I considered taking my trumpet instructor's advice to turn my trumpet into a decorative lamp and go to work in a steel mill.

Fear immobilizes us and keeps us from moving on into God's purposes for our lives. Fear is rooted in our lack of understanding our security in the love of God. As a result, we feel alone and destabilized by the slightest concern. We have pain in the past, we feel paralysis in the present, and we are petrified of the future.

Cautious, Indecisive

When we are under the influence of fear, we live under a sense of dread and desperation. We walk through life taking short, cautious steps, suspicious of everyone and everything. We expect no grace from anyone and cannot afford to extend any either.

Fear makes us live from one choppy, tentative step to the next. We are afraid to make a decision because we might make the wrong one. We are in fear of new relationships because we might get hurt. Therefore, whether it's a new relationship or a new revelation of God, we find it difficult to move ahead. Our tentative steps may be the echo of a parent telling us we can't ever do anything right, so we don't do anything for fear of making mistakes. No decision seems safer than the wrong one. Whatever the source, fear becomes a drag on us that keeps us from enjoying life in all its fullness.

The fear that controls us today, with all its effects, is rooted in the past. It may be the result of a single painful event or the climate of a dysfunctional home. Much of our friend Jacob's fear in the present was rooted in the legalistic and graceless brand of religion that was a part of his early life. Jacob's fear was based on a wrong idea of God. He came to see God as far off and interested only in avenging every infraction of His stringent laws. Healing came when Jacob learned the truth that God had not and would not leave him alone. Neither will He leave any of us alone.

The Truth about Fear

So He said, "Go forth, and stand on the mountain before the Lord." And behold, the Lord was passing by! And a great and strong wind was rending the mountains and breaking in pieces the rocks before the Lord; but the Lord was not in the wind. And after the wind an earthquake, but the Lord was not in the earthquake. And after the earthquake a fire, but the Lord was not in the fire; and after the fire a sound of a gentle blowing. And it came about when Elijah heard it, that he wrapped his face in his mantle, and went out and stood in the entrance of the cave. And behold, a voice came to him and said, "What are you doing here, Elijah?" (1 Kings 19:11-13)

"I am alone...." The words fell limply from Elijah's mouth as the prophet of God sat in the cave on God's mountain. No sooner had the reverberation of his words left the cold walls of his hiding place than he heard the sound of a strong wind blowing past the mouth of the cave. The sound was deafening. Soon, however, the sound seemed to intensify, shaking the ground in an earthquake.

"Lord, is that You?" Elijah said in his raised, quivering voice. But no reply came forth. Then the earthquake was joined by a fire from Heaven, like the fire Elijah himself had called down only days before. "Is that You—Lord?!" Elijah's voice now raised to a shout. "Is that You?" Nothing. He put his hands over his ears to shut out the sound.

When the natural and supernatural disturbance was at its peak—when it seemed that it could not get any louder—a sound began to seep through the bluster. It was faint, but as definite as the sound of a single violin playing a high sustained note above the din of a full orchestra. The sound seemed to grow, not louder, but more prominent as it continued. Eventually it was transformed into a breathy whisper that seemed to distract all of Elijah's attention from the storm—so much so that it caused him to stand up, uncover his ears, and step into the mouth of the cave to hear it better. It was as if the storm of his inner turmoil was being engulfed—embraced—in softness. The sound, as it drowned out the storm, was like that sound he had heard a hundred mothers utter to their crying babies. It was as though Elijah heard the sound of God's voice gently whispering, "Shhhhhh, Elijah. It will be okay. I am here...I am here...Shhhhhhh."

We Are Not Alone

As Elijah sat alone and afraid in the wilderness, the strong hands of a faithful and loving Father picked him up as one would a crying child and lifted him to His heart. Then, as Elijah was hiding in the cave, God answered his fear. God sent the strong wind, earthquake, and fire as signs of the inner turmoil of Elijah's heart—the result of fear that had blocked his view of God. But God was not in any of these. Once the fear of Elijah's heart was stirred, God sent the "sound of a gentle blowing" (1 Kings 19:12) to Elijah; the same sound that your mother or father would make to quiet you when you woke up afraid and alone in the dark. It's a sound of comfort that God speaks to us in those places of darkness and fear:

"Shhh, it's okay—everything will be all right. Daddy's here now. Don't be afraid."

When we run as far and hard as we can, we learn that the presence of God is already ahead of us and ready to pour out His mercy and grace. It was not a surprise that Elijah ran. God knew he was afraid. When Elijah reached the middle of the wilderness, he was met by the mercy of God in the form of a shade tree under which God provided an angel with food and water. Elijah was not left alone in his fear.

When God picked up Elijah as a Father would pick up a crying child and took him to His heart, Elijah's complaint—the source of his fear—was in his statement, "I am alone." The truth was and is that we are not alone, no matter what the circumstance.

God, through His representatives, told us more than 300 times in the Scriptures not to be afraid. There is a "fear not" for every day of the year and every kind of circumstance we encounter. There was a "fear not" before Israel entered into the Promised Land. There was a "fear not" before God used Gideon to deliver Israel from the enemy. There was a "fear not" before Jesus was implanted by the Spirit in the womb of Mary. Throughout the Bible these "fear nots" came to assure those who received them that God's presence was with them even in the midst of great change or challenge. It was their assurance that God would not leave them alone in the dark.

The promise of God's presence was given to the nation of Israel many times when they faced the possibility of danger. As they crossed the frontiers of promise God told them, "The Lord is the one who goes ahead of you; He will be with you. He will not fail you or forsake you. Do not fear or be dismayed" (Deut. 31:8), and "Have I not commanded you? Be strong and courageous! Do not tremble or be dismayed, for the Lord your God is with you wherever you go" (Josh. 1:9). When Israel was taken into captivity, God assured them that even in that place they were not alone. " 'But as for you, O Jacob My servant, do not fear, nor be dismayed, O Israel! For, see, I am going to save you from afar, and your descendants from the land of their captivity; and Jacob will return and be undisturbed and secure, with no one making him tremble. O Jacob My servant, do not fear,' declares the Lord, 'For I am with you' " (Jer. 46:27-28a).

Here the Lord is making a connection between our fears and His presence. God's strategy to protect or heal us from fear is to tell us that

He is "with us." Many times in our ministry I have heard people who live in fear say that they were alone in a time of abuse. Invariably God brought healing to them by showing them in some way that He was, in fact, always there with them and that they were never alone. Somehow the light of God's presence with them dispelled the fear that had controlled them, in some cases, for decades.

Being healed from a controlling fear is a matter of recognizing and appropriating the presence of God whether in the present or in the context of past memories. If we are going to deal with the issue of fear, we must trace it to its root in our own past and allow the presence of God to debunk the lie that we were alone in our fear. We are not beyond God's presence in any place or any time. God will manifest His healing presence in our past just as He did when He showed Himself to that little boy under the bed. Again, we cannot change the event that caused the fear; that is history. But when we recognize that God did not leave us alone, the destructive and controlling influence of fear is destroyed.

Christ Was Alone So We Would Never Be

God the Father, knowing that the fear of being alone was the greatest issue, sent His Son Jesus to be "with us" and heal us of controlling fear. As the Gospel of Matthew says, " 'Behold, the virgin shall be with child and shall bear a Son, and they shall call His name Immanuel,' which translated means, 'God with us' " (Mt. 1:23). Jesus took all of our fear and aloneness to the cross and was Himself alone and forsaken by the Father for a moment so that you and I would never fear being alone again (see Mt. 27:46).

God will meet us in our fear: past, present, and future. When we are afraid, God will meet us and speak to our hearts, saying, "Shhh, I am here, and everything is okay. Don't be afraid." It is a sound that will cut through the strongest fear.

(See *Altars of the Heart Personal Ministry Guide*)

Getting the Picture

Do you ever feel like Elijah did when he was afraid? When have you felt alone, afraid, nervous, paralyzed, tentative, indecisive, worried, or wanting to run away or hide under a bed?

Can you describe a recent time when you felt the things described above? Write a brief description in the picture frame. Before you begin to write, acknowledge the presence and involvement of God through prayer. Do not proceed until you have bathed in prayer and His presence. Declare the intention of the Lord to bring you truth and healing and forbid any lies or interference from unclean spirits.

Describe what you were feeling in that recent event.

Now, pray that the Lord would lead you to the source of those feelings. Ask Him to take you by the hand and lead you to a memory that feels like the recent event you described. Describe the memory picture in the frame below as you did with the recent event. (Note that there may be more than one. Try to find the oldest memory.)

Ask the Lord to fill the memory with His presence. Describe how you experience the presence of God in that picture.

_____

_____

_____

_____

Once you have begun to experience the presence of God ask yourself the following questions. What are you feeling as you look at this memory frame? Why do you feel that way? What did you believe about that event? What does the Lord seem to be telling you about the truth of that situation? How does this frame look now in view of the presence of God?

I believed: _____

But the truth is: _____

Cleaning the House: Forgive, release as led of the Spirit.

What was true in the past is true in the present and will be God's promise to you in the future. Now revisit the present situation you cited at the beginning of this exercise. How do you see it now in light of what God has shown you?

The truth in the past was:_____

The truth in the present is: _____

God's promise to me for the future is: _____

Chapter Seven

WHAT IS YOUR NAME?

Rejection

*When He got out of the boat, immediately a man from the
tombs with an unclean spirit met Him, and he had his dwelling
among the tombs. And no one was able to bind him anymore,
even with a chain; because he had often been bound with
shackles and chains, and the chains had been torn apart by him
and the shackles broken in pieces, and no one was strong
enough to subdue him. Constantly, night and day, he was
screaming among the tombs and in the mountains, and gashing
himself with stones (Mark 5:2-5).*

*And when He came out onto the land, He was met by a man
from the city who was possessed with demons; and who had not
put on any clothing for a long time, and was not living in a
house, but in the tombs (Luke 8:27).*

The Portrait of Rejection

An unnamed man roams through the darkness in the place of the
dead as if searching for something on those tomb markers, his jagged
restlessness punctuated only by the cries of his mournful displacement.
His unsteady hands grope from tomb to tomb, feeling the sharpness of
cold stones bruising his unshod feet. A shiver as lifeless as the moon that
illuminated his staggering, gnome-like figure cut through his uncovered
body, reminding him that he was abandoned to the dead—alone in his
own body.

Jangling remnants of chains and shackles cut deeply into his flesh,
increasing his torment with each movement. A kind of painful emptiness
surrounded him. In his emptiness, this man from the tombs cut himself

with the flinty edges of sharp stones as if to try to focus a pain that de-fied description. And his anger rivaled that of a wild animal whose life was held in captivity—pitiful and unprotected in a place of deafening silence.

Then, with the first rays of dawn's light at his back, he spotted a boat drifting toward the shore of the small sea by which he lived. *Why would a fishing boat come in with the last minutes of darkness?* Fishing boats went out in the morning; they didn't come in. The recluse tightly squinted his eyes to see whom this could be encroaching upon his exile among the dead. As he watched, the small, plain vessel floated to shore off a sea as still and as smooth as glass, its bow coming gently to rest on the dry land.

Something within the man from the tombs at once became unsettled—bereft of its security. There was something magnetic about the otherwise unexceptional figure who stepped out of the boat across its bow. As the man from the boat approached, the morning light from behind the anon-ymous wanderer's back began to reveal the face of the man from the boat. As the dawning sun rose upon that face, all that was within the roam-ing man sensed a presence he had longed to feel—an antidote for his disincorporation—a something to fill his nothingness. The demonic lies that held him bound began to tremble at the appearance of the Son of the Most High.

The Influence of Rejection

The lie believed by those who live under rejection is, "*I do not be-long.*" The rejected ask, "Who am I? Where do I belong? How do I fit in?" The man from the tombs lived in the Gergasenes, the other side of the sea from where Jesus lived. This was the place of the Girgashites. Both words stem from the Hebrew root *ger*, which is the word for a so-journer or stranger. Many people live their lives under this influence. They live like those who hung out on the periphery of the camp of Israel as outsiders. They are the *rejected*.

Rejection is a fact of life played out every day in most every life. When I was a kid, we played baseball almost every day. The kids in the neighborhood hung their baseball mitts over the handlebars of their bi-cycles and converged on the nearest field or schoolyard any day there was no school or when there was no snow on the ground. When there were enough players, two captains would toss a baseball bat back and forth in a ritual that would decide who got the first pick of the other kids to be on their teams. One after the other, players were selected from the most athletic to the least. The greatest fear was to be selected last or perhaps not at all. As the lines of available players grew shorter, those still remaining sank into a kind of resignation of "lastness." That feeling of being last—of being somehow less acceptable or desirable than others—left an impression on those at the end of the line. Many times I was one of those.

We all experience rejection simply because we are not good at everything. The one who was the first baseball player selected may be at the end of the line for the debating team or the last one you would pick to balance your checkbook. Many people today wander from one line to the next, trying to be picked higher in the order than the last line they found. Those who live in such rejection say to themselves, "I am not acceptable...I do not belong...I don't fit in...," or words to that effect. They are the kids in school who are taller, shorter, fatter, thinner, or just different. The key word is *different.*

Rejection is the result of an imperfect or conditional love. It is a love that says, "I will love you if you are worth it to me." This imperfect love leads to great fear of not being accepted by others. Why is this such an issue? God created us to live in community, and He said that it is not good for us to be alone (see Gen. 2:18). Community, belonging to one another, is a strong instinct within us. We are created in community, reflecting the very schematic of God Himself, who exists as a community of sorts: Father, Son, and Holy Spirit. Thus we all were made for each other. If we do not experience that belonging, we wither and die.

Those who feel rejection are those who live on the fringes of the camp in an uneasy truce with those who live closer to the fire, so to speak. They live in the cold outer darkness away from the fire, existing on the scraps of attention thrown to them by the people closer to the fire—by those who seem to be less *different* than they.

The tomb wanderer was the picture of a man who lived in rejection. As we look at his existence, a portrait emerges of those who live in rejection as he did. We don't know what was responsible for his state, but he seems typical of others who find themselves on the outside looking in at life, trying to discover who they are and where they fit in.

There are several aspects in this picture that describe others who live under the influence of rejection. I will be interpreting these passages of

Scripture in a very literal way as a conversation between Jesus and one rejected man, for he lived like many others under the influence of rejection.

Emotional Profile of Rejection

The influence of rejection creates its own emotional profile. Here are a few of the ways the rejected feel.

Separated, Left Out

Many of those who live under the influence of rejection live in a state of separation. The man from the tombs had placed himself where no other person would enter: among the dead. Dead bodies were considered to be unclean and a source of possible defilement for Jewish people. Yet, it seems as though the tomb wanderer was Jewish by the fact that he called Jesus the "Son of the Most High," a term not likely to be used by someone outside the nation of Israel.

Those who live under the influence of rejection tend to pull away from others to avoid being rejected again. They tend to put themselves in places of unavailability, out of the reach of others. They may do so in several different ways. For example, they may separate themselves by building a façade of legalism or piety so as to seem unapproachable. No matter how they pull away, though, they are like the tomb wanderer who placed himself out of the range of others.

Confused

As I stated earlier, I want to interpret this passage in a literal rather than a spiritual way. The man was said to have an "unclean spirit." The Greek word used is *akathartos*, which may be interpreted as a polluted spirit. There is a sort of confusion that surrounds the rejected. Their spirits are polluted by their trying to find acceptance. Imagine the kind of traffic jam that went on in the tomb wanderer's head. Each of hundreds of voices vied for attention and comfort at the same time. He walked about in a confused state, not knowing who or what he was.

We pollute our spirits in many ways by willfully taking on new strategies and disguises to hide our pain. Whatever we take onto ourselves to gain acceptance—other than our acceptance in Christ—is never going to work. Instead these things will become the source of pollution in our own spirits and rob us of true intimacy with God.

Nameless

Rejected people struggle with identity. It is *who* they are that is being denied. This is illustrated in the tomb wanderer's going around with no robe (see Lk. 8:27). The outer robe, or *himation*, was a distinguishing garment bearing the identity of a family. More than an article of clothing, this robe provided a sense of security to the wearer. He lived in it, worked in it, slept in it. It was his life. The fact that the man had no robe demonstrated a lack of identity and security. Without it, as without the unconditional acceptance that we all need, the man lived a cold and anonymous life.

People who live with rejection take on various disguises to gain some kind of acceptable identity. In my younger years I took on the disguise of a "cool musician." When I was very young, my parents noticed that I could whistle a tune or remember a melody sung on a TV commercial. When one of my older brothers left for the Marines in the early 1960s, I borrowed his beaten up old cornet and taught myself to play a little, which got the attention of family and friends. Throughout my school years and long after, I was driven to play music. It became my whole life—the thing I was betting on to keep me out of the darkness and oblivion of rejection. I was a trumpet player. I was fairly good at it and began to play professionally when I was just fifteen years old, playing alongside guys who were in their twenties and thirties or older. It made me feel like I was somebody. But behind the music there was a frightened, rejected kid who just wanted someone to notice he was there. In the end, I was able to make a living playing the trumpet, though it drew me further into isolation and away from God and people.

An individual's identity may be denied in many ways. Perhaps overbearing parents controlled every aspect of a child's life to the point that it crushed his or her sense of identity, leaving the child no room to grow. Or it also could happen if a child has too little attention from parents. Individuals may feel rejected when their parents try to live their lives over again through them, thereby denying their offspring individuality and identity.

Maybe this is why we see children and young adults wearing rings in every body part that can be pierced, dyeing their hair purple, or straining to keep up with the latest styles. They want someone to notice them—to accept them as individuals. They, like the tomb wanderer, are yearning for a way to belong, a way to blend into the crowd, a way to stay close to the fire.

Angry

Rejection, remember, is the result of imperfect love. Love that is imperfect holds some kind of condition or criteria for acceptance. It is a love that makes us conform to someone's arbitrary standard. The man from the tombs had been shackled and chained many times—only to break free and wander off again. Those shackles and chains were an attempt to control how he walked or lived. Probably some well-meaning folks thought that this man's problems could be taken care of if he would just "live like us." Those restraints, however, would have only served to make him feel more rejected—more angry.

His breaking free of those chains and shackles in such great ferocity is a demonstration of anger, which is a big part of rejection. The Bible unfolds a pattern of rejection that leads to anger that leads to death. Cain believed God rejected him, and he became angry and murdered his brother Abel (see Gen. 4:1-8). Esau, deprived of his father's blessing, felt rejected and wanted to kill his brother Jacob (see Gen. 27:34-41). God rejected Saul for his disobedience, and Saul spent the last years of his life chasing David, God's anointed one, to kill him (see 1 Sam. 15:26). Where there is rejection, there is anger and death.

I have noticed in the Bible and in our ministry that such anger is usually pointed at someone whom we feel is more accepted than we are. Tragically, this is probably true of those children who walk into school with guns to blow away those who are the more accepted kids—the cool kids.

For example, kids who were angry and rejected populated the "Trench Coat Mafia" of Columbine High School in Littleton, Colorado. Two of them acted out of their rejection. They made lists of other students whom they saw as more accepted and systematically sought them out to murder them. *Rejection* led to *anger* that led to *death*.

Restless, Unsettled

The man from the tombs was a man crying out "night and day," which is a way of saying that he had no kind of rest. His crying and screaming was more like the cry of a wounded animal calling attention to its pain. Though we have no recording of the words he cried out, his message is clear: "Does anyone see me? Does anyone care?"

The man also gashed himself with sharp stones to increase the volume and intensity of his call, much like the prophets of Baal whose god did not hear them (see 1 Kings 18:28). Those living outside the warmth and glow of the campfire are calling out to be noticed—to be called closer to the fire. They feel forgotten and forsaken. We have ministered many times to the rejected who have harmed themselves in some way. Sometimes they cut themselves; sometimes they starve themselves. The self-hurt seems to be a way for them to be able to cry out louder, for those who feel rejected also feel unheard. They are crying out to belong—to feel a part of something warm and loving.

The Truth about Rejection

And seeing Jesus from a distance, he ran up and bowed down before Him; and crying out with a loud voice, he said, "What do I have to do with You, Jesus, Son of the Most High God? I implore You by God, do not torment me!" For He had been saying him, "Come out of the man, you unclean spirit!" And He was asking him, "What is your name?" And he said to Him, "My name is Legion; for we are many." And he began to entreat Him earnestly not to send them out of the country. Now there was a big herd of swine feeding there on the mountain. And the demons entreated Him, saying, "Send us into the swine so that we may enter them." And He gave them permission. And coming out, the unclean spirits entered the swine; and the herd rushed down the steep bank into the sea, about two thousand of them; and they were drowned in the sea. And their herdsmen ran away and reported it in the city and out in the country. And the people came to see what it was that had happened. And they came to Jesus and observed the man who had been demon-possessed sitting down, clothed and in his right mind, the very man who had had the "legion"; and they became frightened (Mark 5:6-15).

A thousand episodes of emptiness flooded the tomb wanderer's memory. As the illumined figure from the boat stood before him, the wanderer threw himself at Jesus' feet. A voice rose up out of the loneliness of the man's heart, shattering the silence between them and giving expression to the pain in the wanderer's heart. "What do we have to do with one another—who are You—who am I? Don't torment me anymore—don't play games with me, Son of the Most High. Don't give me another sermon...I don't need three steps to acceptability. I need to be warm—to be close. I need to know, do You accept me? Do You have a place for me?"[8]

Now, in this most pregnant moment, a gentle voice issued from the mouth of the Man from the boat, His words striking deep into the heart of the solitary man from the tombs: "What is your name?" The question reverberated in the man's mind, stirring a thousand voices wanting to respond. "I am a legion of names—I have tried everything to get close." But now, looking up into the face of Jesus, the tomb wanderer's heart became still—just as the sea had done only hours earlier at the voice of Jesus (see Mk. 4:35-41). The question and the answer both issued from the same mouth.

Jesus had come to the place of this man's darkness and rejection. It was for *him* that Jesus left His home. It was for *him* that Jesus fought seas, conquered storms, and brought peace. It was for *him* that Jesus sailed through the darkness to this lonely desolate place of the dead. There could be no stronger words of acceptance.

With his eyes full of the face of Jesus, words were not needed. In His coming, Jesus had answered the man's desperate inquiry, "Who am I?

---

8.   Note that my interpretation of this passage is very literal. The man was obviously filled with demonic presence but they all spoke through the man's mouth. I am interpreting in a way that shows the response of those living under the influence of rejection, not to in any way deny the demonic that was so apparently present in the man. A careful reading of the text indicates that Jesus was speaking to the man and that the demons answered through the man's mouth. Note the use of the masculine singular in the text. The "*he*" in verse 7 is the man.

"*Seeing Jesus from a distance, **he** ran up and bowed down before Him; and shouting with a loud voice, **he** said, 'What business do we have with each other, Jesus, Son of the Most High God? I implore You by God, do not torment **me**!' For He had been saying to **him**, 'Come out of the man, you unclean spirit!' And He was asking him, 'What is **your** name?' And he said to Him, '**My** name is Legion; for we are many'* " (Mk. 5:6-9).

Who are You?" Implicitly Jesus was saying, "You are the one I have come for—for *you*! You belong to Me! That is who you are. Here is where you belong!"

With that gesture, Jesus walked up to every wallflower who had ever been, or ever would be, and said, "Who are *you*? I want to know *you*—yes, *you*!"

With the truth declared, the demons inside the man—his many ideas about himself and his attempts to find acceptance—had to flee to the nearest swine. Once truth comes and the lies are displaced, the forces of hell have no legal place to stand and must therefore go. And they went!

The truth now announced for the world to hear, the man's restless wandering ceased. His friends found this formerly tormented man sitting down, no longer wandering. He was wearing a new robe, clothed with the name of the One who came just for him, and able to truthfully relate to God and the world. He was in his right mind—he had a new revelation of who he was in the face of Jesus Christ (see Mk. 5:15).

We Are Accepted in Christ

There is no night too dark, no shore too distant, for the presence and compassion of God. There was no other purpose for Jesus on that shore that day; no other ministry event was recorded in that place. Jesus came just for this man to bring him to Himself. The simple truth about rejection that we have heard uttered time and time again in ministry sessions is that we are who we are in Christ Jesus. We are defined and identified solely by our relationship with Him. We are who He says we are, not who the world says we are.

It is impossible for God to forget us or to ignore us. As the prophet says, "Remember these things, O Jacob, and Israel, for you are My servant; I have formed you, you are My servant, O Israel, you will not be forgotten by Me" (Is. 44:21). To those of you who have lived on the edge of the camp, in the outer cold away from the fire, God has brought the fire to you. You are no longer outsiders, but the ultimate insiders: inside the heart of God.

The Psalmist writes prophetically of Jesus, who would suffer the ultimate rejection and injustice of the cross:

My God, my God, why have You forsaken me? Far from my deliverance are the words of my groaning. O my God, I cry by day, but You do not answer; and by night, but I have no rest (Psalm 22:1-2).

It was Christ who was forsaken; the Father's back was to Him. It was Jesus who groaned in the pain of utter aloneness and separation from the Father. It was Jesus who cried out in the pain of rejection so that we would not have to. It was Jesus who knew the unrelenting torment and restless condition of the cross so that you and I would be able to rest in His finished work. It was Jesus who was despised and rejected of men who hid their faces from Him (see Is. 53:3).

We are made acceptable by the blood of Jesus alone. "He saved us, not on the basis of deeds which we have done in righteousness, but according to His mercy" (Tit. 3:5a). We have been "accepted in the beloved [Jesus]" (Eph. 1:6 KJV). It is an acceptance that is incorruptible and unconditional. No one can take it away from us, and it will never be out of style.

In our acceptance we can now risk the company of others who may or may not accept us. The man among the tombs to whom Jesus had taken this message of acceptance wanted to jump into the boat with Jesus to follow Him. Jesus instructed him, however, to go back home—probably to the very ones who rejected him—to bring word of God's goodness to him. The man did as Jesus instructed and those who saw him and knew him were amazed at the mercy of God. We are accepted by the Lord Jesus who has come for us, and out of that acceptance we can accept those others.

Our Identity Is in Christ

What is your name? Who are you? Where do you belong? Jesus gives us a new identity and therefore a new and incorruptible acceptance. It is possible that others may have turned their backs on us, but Jesus stands with arms open wide to receive us. Jesus has set sail to reach the rejected—He has calmed the raging sea and sailed through the darkness just for you. He left His own comfort and crossed a storm-tossed blackness to walk right into our rejection so that we could be healed by His presence.

As you read these very words, know that the living and ascended Christ has come for you. The boat has set sail. He has calmed the sea and has come for you. Who He says you are is who you are!

(See *Altars of the Heart Personal Ministry Guide*)

Getting the Picture

Does your life look like that of the man from the tombs? Do you feel separated, left out, angry, rejected, forsaken (like someone has turned his back on you), an outsider, forgotten, restless, nameless? Take a moment and compare the picture of the life of the man from the tombs with your life. Before you begin to write, acknowledge the presence and involvement of God through prayer. Do not proceed until you have bathed in prayer and His presence. Declare the intention of the Lord to bring you truth and healing and forbid any lies or interference from unclean spirits.

Describe a recent time when you felt the things described above.

_____

_____

_____

_____

_____

_____

Now, pray that the Lord would lead you to the source of those feelings. Ask Him to take you by the hand and lead you to a memory that feels like the recent event you described. This will be a root memory. Describe the memory picture in the frame below as you did with the recent event.

_____

_____

_____

_____

_____

_____

What are you feeling as you look at this memory picture? Why do you feel what you feel? What did you believe about that event? Now pray for the Lord to show you what is true.

I believed: _____

But the truth is: _____

Cleaning the House: Forgive, release as led of the Spirit.

What was true in the past is true in the present and will be God's promise to you in the future. Now revisit the present situation you cited at the beginning of this exercise. How do you see it now in light of what God has shown you?

The truth in the past was: _____

The truth in the present is: _____

God's promise to me for the future is: _____

Chapter Eight

LIVING IN SECOND PLACE

Worthlessness

Now Laban had two daughters: Leah, who was the oldest, and her younger sister, Rachel. Leah had pretty eyes, but Rachel was beautiful in every way, with a lovely face and shapely figure (Genesis 29:16-17 NLT).

The Portrait of Worthlessness

She had pretty eyes, did Leah. She was a pleasant and mature young woman prepared in her role as the older daughter of Laban to take up responsibility for running the household. Leah was responsible for her younger sister Rachel from the time she was an infant, and she learned everything there was to know about maintaining home and family. Leah had ripened on the vine of Laban's house. She was the best that Laban had to offer.

Now Jacob had come into her father's house. He was a handsome and talented man, and everything he touched seemed to turn to gold. Jacob was an infusion of new blood into the family. It seemed natural to everyone that a merger should take place between the house of Laban and the grandson of Abraham. What better way to bring the two houses together than through the union of Laban's oldest daughter and the son of Isaac? It just made sense.

The oldest daughter of Laban was thrilled at the prospect of marriage. The preparations were made and the invitations sent. Like any other girl of her time, she dreamed of setting up her own home and raising her own family. The day had been fixed for the wedding feast, and she began to make preparations for a new life. Now the day of building her own house had come.

The feast was loud and joyous, and the whole neighborhood showed up. All of her friends and neighbors were there to witness the joining of the two houses. The food and the celebration seemed endless. Everyone had a great time. When the celebration was over, Leah was brought to the tent where her marriage with Jacob would be consummated. She was brought to her husband in a veil that covered her from head to toe, obscuring not only her pretty eyes but also her form. The time had come—a new era had begun in her life.

Then came the morning after. The party was over, and there was only the stillness and grog of the next day. As she awakened, the new bride looked into the face of her husband, thrilled with the prospect of married life. As her husband awoke, he looked into her pretty eyes, but instead of delight there was a look of surprise and betrayal. His eyes opened wider as he looked at her in disbelief. Sitting up suddenly, Jacob quickly grabbed something to cover himself and sprang from his bed. "What's this? What are you doing here? You were not the one I wanted, not the one I worked for."

She was somehow a disappointment—less than he expected—worth less than her sister. Leah was thrust into a place that she had never planned and didn't deserve. She was living in second place.

The Lie of Worthlessness

Think about it for a minute. How would you feel if you woke up on the day after your wedding with your spouse telling you that you were a disappointment, that he wanted someone else—your own sister? Such was the case with Leah, who lived under the influence of worthlessness. The lie of worthlessness is *"I am not as good"*—that our worth is determined by comparison to someone else. We see ourselves in terms of everybody else, and we spend our lives chasing some kind of ideal that doesn't exist anywhere but in the heads of those who feel worth *less*.

Worthlessness is the influence of the Amorites. The root of the name *Amorite* comes from the word that means to speak or declare something. In this case we are referring to things spoken over us that do not agree with the purpose or the promises of God. It was the Amorites who opposed the progression of God's people into the land of promise. They stood against the nation of Israel and the word of God (see Num. 21:21-35).

The lie of worthlessness declares that we are worth less than God said. Those who live under the influence of worthlessness feel devalued as they compare themselves to other people.

The world, and dare I say even the Church, has created a prototype of perfection that makes us feel guilty for not looking like the people on magazine covers. We are compared to the tall, the rich, the smart—the prom queens and football captains. Everyone has to be young, white, thin, rich…you name it. If we don't conform, we become invisible and unimportant to those who compare more favorably, or who at least think they do.

Anyone who does not conform to the prototype is dismissed to the nerd table in the cafeteria. They are like the rest of the wolves in the pack who live below the Alpha, or dominant, pair. In truth, most of us are somewhere down the alphabet from the Alphas of the world. We are not wolves, but we live like them, ready to snarl our disapproval of those on the fringes of the pack. Yes, there is a trend even among the saints of God to value others by the kind of car that they park in the parking lot on Sunday morning or by the amount of the tithe they bring.

Life in second place has its destructive and limiting effects on us. As we look at Leah's life, a picture emerges that describes the Betas (those who believe they are in second place) who live in lesser places—who feel worth *less* than the Alphas of the world.

Leah had weak or "pretty eyes," as the New Living Translation puts it. She didn't have the dark, passionate eyes that were so admired among the ancient Middle Eastern people. She didn't stand out alongside her sister, who was said to be beautiful in form and figure. She was just an average person, like most of us. Many today who live under this influence of comparison spend their lives trying to achieve that magazine cover perfection.

The truth is that most of us are average and will not appear any time soon on a movie screen, yet we still look to the world for approval that is, at best, fleeting. That approval will disappear along with our hair and youthful form. Whatever appeals to the world will sag or wear out sooner or later. Worldly approval is fleeting.

As we look at Leah's life, a picture emerges of those who believe they are worthless. Even the names Leah gave to her children demonstrate something of how she felt. Taken together, they present a vivid portrait of those who believe themselves to be worth less than someone else.

Emotional Profile of Worthlessness

Those who live under the influence of worthlessness feel like Leah felt. They believe they are unloved.

Unloved

The first and greatest effect of the lie of worthlessness is the belief that we are unloved, or perhaps more accurately, that we are loved *less*. In some sense, we believe that we are less lovable than someone else. Leah believed that her first two sons were God's response to the fact that she was unloved.

> *Now the Lord saw that Leah was **unloved**, and He opened her womb, but Rachel was barren. Leah conceived and bore a son and named him Reuben, for she said, "Because the Lord has seen my affliction; surely now my husband will love me." Then she conceived again and bore a son and said, "Because the Lord has heard that I am unloved, He has therefore given me this son also." So she named him Simeon* (Genesis 29:31-33).

It was not that Leah was not loved at all, but that she was not loved the same way her sister was loved. She was the good and responsible daughter of Laban. She was like the girl whom everyone wanted as a friend in study hall but would not ask to the prom. It wasn't that Leah was not loved, but that she was not the love of someone's life. She was not special.

Unnoticed

The names of her first two sons, Reuben and Simeon, describe her feelings of being ignored—*unnoticed*. Leah declared that in giving birth to her first son Reuben (meaning, "see a son," or perhaps "you see a son"), God had seen her "affliction" or humiliation. Imagine how Leah must have felt seeing her husband go into the tent of her younger sister, the one she helped to raise.

Leah's second son, Simeon, whose name comes from the word for hearing, adds to her belief that no one noticed her for who she was—no one but God, that is. Those who live under the influence of this lie of worthlessness live a life in the shadows of the beautiful people. They are like the girl who stands alongside the head cheerleader, unnoticed. The

Leahs of the world are the ones who do their jobs and seldom complain. They believe themselves to be ordinary, unexceptional people.

Unattached

The birth of two sons did not buy any self-worth for Leah. She would strive to have another son: Levi.

She conceived again and bore a son and said, "Now this time my husband will become attached to me, because I have borne him three sons." Therefore he was named Levi (Genesis 29:34).

We are created to feel attached to other humans. We have a designed need for connectedness. There is a sense of emptiness when we don't experience the kind of emotional heart attachment we need. Leah tried to perform her way into an emotional bond with Jacob.

Leah's son's name, Levi, could be interpreted as "my attachment." Having another son was her ticket to the warmth of her husband. Leah, like others who live under the influence of worthlessness, experienced conditional love in her connection to other people. Such individuals feel that they must do something to earn that love, whether it's hitting a baseball for Dad or scoring 1400 on SAT tests. They are not worth the love in themselves.

Once again, Leah had another son, Judah. With the birth of this son she felt free to praise God. This son is the one for whom Jehovah is praised. She says, "This time I will praise the Lord" (Gen. 29:35). Now she shifted to the means by which she gained attachment. I have heard people many times being praised or approved for some physical aspect of beauty or some "anointing" they are perceived to have. Although this sounds like genuine praise, it is once again conditioned on something.

Jealous

Those who don't experience the intimacy of affection and approval look with longing and envy at those who do. The biblical text indicates that Leah believed that Jacob was her husband and that Rachel stole him. When Rachel asked for the mandrake roots gathered by Leah's son, Leah replied, "Is it a small matter for you to take my husband?" (Gen. 30:15). Her question to Rachel not only verifies that she believed herself to be the intended wife of Jacob, but also points out that those who believe they are worth less tend to be jealous of those who have more.

Those who live under worthlessness spend their time looking to see who got the bigger piece of the pie. The result is that they seldom are satisfied with the piece of the pie they have. They don't see that sometimes those who get the bigger slice get a stomachache. They grow weary in comparison and are never satisfied even in their relationship with God. Someone will always be smarter, prettier, taller, or thinner, and those under worthlessness always envy him or her.

Unworthy

People who don't feel they compare well with others will spend their time trying to prove their worth. Leah's name means "wearied." The name fits, since she spent her life trying to prove her worth to her husband by having children.

The name and the account of Issachar's birth give us a picture of love bought. Leah actually purchased the love and affections of her husband with a few mandrake roots. She tells Jacob, "You must come in to me, for I have surely hired you with my son's mandrakes" (Gen. 30:16). Leah believed that she had to purchase the love of her husband.

Others of us may not purchase a night in the honeymoon suite with mandrake roots, but we still pay for the love and acceptance of other people. We may pay this bill by endless activity or works done to get noticed or feel worthwhile. But eventually morning will come and Jacob will get up and go back to Rachel's tent. At the end of the day we will still feel empty—unworthy.

Unapproved

With the birth of Zebulun, Leah proclaimed that she had now presented a sufficient dowry for her husband. Bear in mind that she had already given Jacob five sons herself and two more by her servant. It seemed that no matter what she did, she still lacked a sense of final approval and acceptance from her husband. This seems to sum up the belief of those under the influence of worthlessness: No matter what they do, no matter how hard they try, they never find approval.

Carolyn was a vibrant, youthful woman in her mid-forties who, despite her great love of God and her many gifts for ministry and personal affability, never seemed to be able to come to the point of satisfaction with her life. She was tormented by the feeling that she could never do enough things or do them well enough. This seemed to go against common sense and appearances because she was first at everything. She was a home-coming queen and a top student—one of the "Alphas" of the world. But somehow she was still empty. Carolyn came from a strong Christian family with her father being a career military man. She had always gotten good grades and done what good girls do, but nothing she ever did satisfied her.

As we prayed together, the Lord allowed her to remember a time when she was in her late twenties and playing in a women's competitive softball league. She was a good athlete who had a strong love of the Lord and for her family. In this memory frame Carolyn was playing in a game and got a good hit that came at a crucial time in the game. When the girl who followed her in the batting order also got a hit, Carolyn scored a run. It was all very exciting.

The first thing that Carolyn wanted to do when she crossed home plate was to go into the stands to find her father, who had come to see her play in the game. She found him sitting behind the dugout and ran over to him excited about what she had done. When she got to him, he was smiling and happy to see her. But when she got next to him, he said something like this: "Well, Peanut, if you would have widened your batting stance a little, you might have gotten a better hit." She was crushed like a beach ball run over by a truck. She had not come to him for batting tips; she wanted his approval and affection and for him to share in her excitement.

It was clear that Carolyn believed that no matter what she did in any area of life, it would never be as good as what someone else did. She would never find approval. She had lived under the influence of the lie of worthlessness. As we continued to pray, we asked the Lord Himself to reveal the truth to her. Immediately, the image of a picture came to mind with Jesus standing behind a small child at home plate in a baseball game. Jesus was smiling in the picture, just enjoying being with the child, and the child had not done anything yet. He was just standing at the plate!

The message was clear: The Lord was pleased with the child and with Carolyn regardless of how well she did something. His hands were on the bat with hers, and He was having fun and enjoying her. The lie of worthlessness was deflated as her ego had been a few moments earlier. We praised God and wept for His love toward her as His special child.

The Truth about Worthlessness

We Are God's Workmanship

The truth regarding the lie of worthlessness is that there is no second place. God does not compare us with any other person. We are handmade originals. We are not cheap, mass-produced fiddles from the wholesale house; we are Stradivarius violins, priceless and incomparable even to another Stradivarius. Have you heard of these violins? *Antonius* Stradivarius made what are now the hallmark of all violins in the 1600–1700s. Even now, hundreds of years later, they are still considered to be the greatest ever built.

As far as I know, there were no second-rate Stradivarius violins. There was no instrument in second place. Each original that was ever made by maestro Stradivarius' hand had a quality of its own. He hand-picked the wood for each one. The oil of his own hands was impregnated in the aged wooden parts. Though the sound was unique in each instrument, each one sang out the praise of its maker.

In the same way, the only comparison that we can make is that we are incomparable to any other person ever made. We are as original and unique as our fingerprints.

The Word of God is clear on who made us:

Know that the Lord Himself is God; it is He who has made us, and not we ourselves; we are His people and the sheep of His pasture. Enter His gates with thanksgiving and His courts with praise. Give thanks to Him, bless His name. For the Lord is good; His lovingkindness is everlasting and His faithfulness to all generations (Psalm 100:3-5).

For You formed my inward parts; You wove me in my mother's womb. I will give thanks to You, for I am fearfully and wonderfully made; wonderful are Your works, and my soul knows it very well (Psalm 139:13-14).

Thus says the Lord, your Redeemer, and the one who formed you from the womb, "I, the Lord, am the maker of all things" (Isaiah 44:24a).

For we are His workmanship, created in Christ Jesus for good works, which God prepared beforehand so that we would walk in them (Ephesians 2:10).

As God's irreplaceable and handmade creations, we cannot be compared to any other. We belong to Him.

We Are Precious

Each of us is a special creation of God. What is important to God seldom appears important to man. God does not see things in the carnal comparative way that we do, any more than we see our own children in that way.

Although both Leah and Rachel bore children who were important to the nation of Israel, it was Leah who brought forth the firstborn son of Jacob, Reuben, and it was from her son Judah that the Messiah of the world would descend. It was from Leah that the Levitical priesthood would spring forth. And finally, it was Leah who was buried alongside her husband, not Rachel (see Gen. 49:29-33).

God Does Not Compare Us

"...God sees not as man sees, for man looks at the outward appearance, but the Lord looks at the heart" (1 Samuel 16:7).

God is not concerned about the world's opinion or judgment of us. The Lord does not always use the people who are the most talented, beautiful, or gifted; rather, He uses those people in whom He has developed character. Think about Leah, Moses, David, and Jesus. In fact, Jesus was nothing special in appearance; He was an average-looking Joshua (see Is. 53:2).

God is more concerned with the heart. Leah had a heart to fear the Lord. She was not party to the superstition of her father's idols as Rachel was, who stole them (see Gen. 31:19). It was Leah, the one with the pretty eyes, who loved the Lord.

The Picture of Truth

The truth about worthlessness is summed up in a picture that arose during a ministry session with Corrine. Now, Corrine was the middle one of three sisters. All three sisters were beautiful and talented in their own ways, and though they loved one another, they always were comparing themselves to one another.

Corrine was the divorced mother of three children. She described to me her life of busyness and activity, but it was one in which she felt no true satisfaction. She was involved in everything, yet she never felt that she could do enough. Though she was obviously an attractive woman, she constantly compared herself to both of her sisters, finding ways they were better or more worthwhile than she. She compared her appearance and her education to that of her siblings and arrived at the opinion that she really "had nothing to offer."

When the lie of worthlessness was uncovered, the Lord walked her to a memory picture of sitting on the bed behind her older sister, watching the sister brush her own hair. She could see the smiling, lovely face of her sister, but she could not see her own face. She was invisible even to herself. The lie that she believed was that she had nothing to offer—that she was just the middle and unexceptional sister. When she herself spoke the lie, I asked the Lord to manifest the truth to her. I had not even finished my sentence before the Lord gave her an image of Him standing behind *her* and brushing *her* hair. This was the Lord's way of saying, "You are precious and special to Me." Tears came with the truth, as they usually do. Corrine was special—she was the one whose hair was brushed by the Lord Himself. What could be clearer?

The truth is that we are God's creation—His own children. If we do not compare our own children, then why do we compare His? Some of His children have various abilities and facets that sparkle in a unique way— they have pretty eyes. Let's not compare one rare treasure with another.

(See *Altars of the Heart Personal Ministry Guide*)

Getting the Picture

How does the portrait of your own life look like Leah's? Do you live in second place? Are you always working and striving to prove your value? Do you struggle with feelings of being unloved, unnoticed, unattached, jealous, or unworthy? Before you begin to write, acknowledge the presence and involvement of God through prayer. Do not proceed until you have bathed in prayer and His presence. Declare the intention of the Lord to bring you truth and healing and forbid any lies or interference from unclean spirits.

Describe a recent time when you felt the things described above.

Describe what you were feeling during that recent event.

Now, pray that the Lord would lead you to the source of those feelings. Ask Him to take you by the hand and lead you to a memory that feels like the recent event you described. Describe the memory picture in the frame below as you did with the recent event.

What are you feeling as you look at this memory picture? Why do you feel what you feel? (That is the lie you believe about this event, and all others that feel like it.) Now pray for the Lord to show you what is true.

I believed: _____

But the truth is: _____

Cleaning the House: Forgive, release as led of the Spirit.

What was true in the past is true in the present and will be God's promise to you in the future. Now revisit the present situation you cited at the beginning of this exercise. How do you see it now in light of what God has shown you?

The truth in the past was: _____

The truth in the present is: _____

God's promise to me for the future is: _____

Chapter Nine

CRYING OVER SPILLED MILK

Shame

When the woman saw that the tree was good for food, and that it was a delight to the eyes, and that the tree was desirable to make one wise, she took from its fruit and ate; and she gave also to her husband with her, and he ate. Then the eyes of both of them were opened, and they knew that they were naked; and they sewed fig leaves together and made themselves loin coverings. They heard the sound of the Lord God walking in the garden in the cool of the day, and the man and his wife hid themselves from the presence of the Lord God among the trees of the garden (Genesis 3:6-8).

The Portrait of Shame

It was the end of the day and the sun had crossed the pinnacle of the sky. The man and woman had been occupied throughout the day with their work in the garden and were returning to their place of rest. They could already feel the breeze growing cooler. It was fast approaching the time of day when the Creator-Friend came to talk with them.

Now, as she walked through the garden, the woman glanced through the lush green vegetation to see the tree in the midst of Eden, whose fruit was weighed down with juicy sweetness, inviting her to quench her deep thirst and recover from the day's labor. It looked so good, and she could only imagine what it tasted like. But the word from the Creator was clear: "Don't touch this tree; it's bad for you."

The woman, though, couldn't stop looking at the tree. Something told her that it had to be good for them. Why would the Creator-Friend withhold the very best from them? How could something that looked so

103

good be bad? Surely He was mistaken, or maybe they had not heard Him right. It just could not be that they were to leave this tree and its luscious fruit alone.

The woman approached the tree cautiously, the thought of the taste of its fruit overwhelming the words and warnings of the Creator-Friend. She reached out for the fruit with the man standing mute beside her. She pulled the fruit from the tree and took it into her hand. She looked at it for a moment, and then, closing her eyes, bit into the fruit. Its juice filled her mouth and awakened her senses. It was delicious.

The woman handed the fruit to her husband to pass along the experience. He, in turn, bit into the fruit and wiped the excess juice from his lips. But instead of delight, immediately a sick feeling came over them both. The fruit that moments earlier awakened their senses now tasted like the clay they stood on. A brown deadness began to permeate their bodies, beginning with their mouths and radiating throughout to the extremities of their bodies. It was as though the sun went down hours early and life was bleeding out of them with every beat of their hearts.

Finally, they came to an intense reality that they were alone. It was as though flesh had been amputated from the spirit. It was like a fingernail that was cut off and just lying there dead and useless—separate. The intimate connection between flesh and spirit—that realm where God spoke of His love for them—was now blank and void. They were filled with a new sensation—one that they had not known, that no creature had known. It was a feeling of a vacuous and naked aloneness.

Man and woman were suddenly aware that they were disconnected from the Creator. They were puny and vulnerable. Shaken, they grabbed leaves off the trees and hurriedly wove them together to conceal their nakedness. Where their minds had been so able and ready to hear the thoughts of the Creator, now they could hear only the sound of their own accelerated heartbeats and thoughts of sheer terror.

And now came the sound of footsteps…

The Influence of Shame

The lie of shame is "*I am not good enough.*" It is a lie of comparison like worthlessness, but instead of comparing ourselves to other people we compare ourselves to some kind of standard.

There is a common phrase that some parents speak over their own child when he or she does something wrong or something that displeases the parents. The parents may say, "Shame on you." The unfortunate result of this pronouncement is that shame does come upon the child. Shame makes the child recoil and hang his head, not to mention cutting him off from relationship with the parent. Nothing good can happen when we say, "Shame on you." Nothing!

When our girls were small, occasionally they would spill some milk at the table. I think there is some kind of clause in the baby contract that a small child must spill something at the table at least once a day. It is inevitable that toddlers will spill the milk. As parents, we have one of two options as to how we respond. We can either yell something at them that they already know—namely, that they spilled their milk. Or we can grab a towel and clean up the mess.

Our response was, usually (though not always, I'm sorry to say), was to clean up the milk and then deal with the cause, if there was one. If we would have just gone off on them, reminding them that they were careless or stupid for spilling their drink, the milk would have just lain on the table and begun to stink after a few days. The stink of that spilled milk is synonymous with the shame of past sin or shortfalls for which we believe there is no healing or forgiveness. When we are under the influence of shame, we are, in effect, "crying over spilled milk." We are focusing on the mess of the past without seeing the way to clean it up. Shame is the result of "stinkin' thinkin' " about God and His grace. Shame tends to remove us from the very place that God so wants us to be—namely, with Him.

Shame is the Canaanite influence. The Hebrew name *Canaan* suggests humiliation. It was Canaan, the grandson of Noah, whose descendants bore the shame of the sin of looking upon Noah's drunken nakedness following the flood. Shame and nakedness go together throughout the Bible. When we are naked, we are exposed, vulnerable, and defenseless. Our reaction to shame or nakedness is to hide from one another, from God, and even from ourselves.

We need to be clear here that shame is the serpent's idea, not God's. We were created for intimate fellowship with God. Before the Fall, man looked forward to the distinct sound of God's footsteps in the cool of the day because they portended a wonderful fellowship with the

Creator-Friend. But when we live under the influence of shame and hear the sound of God's footsteps, we reach for the nearest fig leaf.

Shame is, above all, the belief that we have crossed over a line that is beyond the grace of God. When we live under the influence of shame, we say to ourselves, "I have gone too far; there is no forgiveness for me." Of course that is a lie. Lines do not limit the love of God.

The love of God is the most sovereign force in the universe. God loves out of His sovereignty without condition because He is God and does not need anything from us. What, after all, can we do for God? What can we give to Him that didn't come from Him in the first place? God declares, "If I were hungry I would not tell you, for the world is Mine, and all it contains" (Ps. 50:12). No line, no sin, can keep God from calling us back to Himself. God won't quit! God is not intimidated by lines I draw in the sand by my sin. Sin may control us sometimes, but it does not control God.

As with the other lies and influences we have discussed, shame results in its own list of effects and feelings.

Emotional Profile of Shame

He said, "I heard the sound of You in the garden, and I was afraid because I was naked; so I hid myself" (Genesis 3:10).

Genesis 3:10 gives us a kind of schematic of shame's effects. Shame begins with some kind of infraction or sin, which leaves us with a feeling of guilt, which leads to self-consciousness, which leads to fear, which leads to covering up and separation.

Guilt

The primary picture of guilt is that of a weight that we carry. One of the New Testament words for guilt, *hupodikos*, implies that we are under or beneath judgment, as if it is weighing on us. David had the same descriptive feelings of his own guilt. "When I kept silent about my sin, my body wasted away through my groaning all day long. For day and night Your hand was heavy upon me; my vitality was drained away as with the fever heat of summer" (Ps. 32:3-4). David was being crushed beneath the burden of unconfessed sin. Shame is the crushing burden of our failure that we carry so unnecessarily.

Guilt in itself is not a bad thing until it crushes and immobilizes us into shame. While guilt is like a burden that can be handed over to the Lord for forgiveness, shame is more like defiling toxic mud—a crazy glue from hell that binds us to sin and prevents us from receiving the Lord's presence and the restoration of forgiveness.

Shame is therefore a blending of guilt and hopelessness that produces death in us. As Paul writes, "For the sorrow that is according to the will of God produces a repentance without regret, leading to salvation, but the sorrow of the world produces death" (2 Cor. 7:10). Guilt is a good and godly thing that can lead us back to God. It is the province of the Holy Spirit who convicts us of sin (see Jn. 16:8). Shame begins when we hide and see no way out of our sin. If we perceive God to be like an unforgiving and detached grandfather who is never pleased, shame will keep us in our guilt and separated from God.

It is important to recognize that we are not always guilty of the things that become sources of shame. We may *feel* guilty because we have not met someone else's expectation, but that does mean we are. Actually, perfectionism is a form of shame. We measure ourselves by a standard and come up wanting. Perfectionists believe that anything short of perfection is unacceptable. They learned that somewhere, usually at home.

I sat with a man one day who remembered bringing home a report card with something like all A-'s. His parents (unlike mine, who would have been delighted and shocked at such a good report) said that if he would just work a little harder, he could get straight A's. He was, to say the least, never able to please his parents.

We have many expectations handed down to us that are not of God. No matter what they are or where they came from, God does not require us to haul our sins around our necks as penance. That is a religious concept, but it is not a God thing.

A number of years ago there was a movie titled *The Mission* in which a conquistador was guilty of killing a man in a sword fight. The man went to the priest and was told to do penance for the death by chaining his armor to himself to represent the guilt of his sin. In this way he could appreciate the weight of what he had done.

There came a time when the man was exhausted with the weight of his sin. Then, as he was climbing a hill and could no longer bear the weight of the sin/armor, he began to fall backward. Just as he was at the end of his strength, someone cut the armor loose, allowing the sin/armor to fall away and free the man. That weight he carried was guilt, but the chain that bound him to it was shame.

Along with a burden of guilt comes the knowledge of our sheer nakedness—our powerlessness over sin.

Self-Consciousness and Hiding

Shame focuses us on whatever is naked and vulnerable. Shame leads us to cover up our weakness or vulnerability. David said that his sin was always before him (see Ps. 51:3). In other words, he was preoccupied with it; it ruled his life. Shame allows us little opportunity to see God because we are so focused on our nakedness. It is a feeling of humiliation and exposure.

When we live under shame we tend to cover up as Adam did by sewing some fig leaves together. Those fig leaves are whatever we can muster to conceal our exposure. They may be our own legalistic system or some kind of works we do in order to feel worthy again. Those works, like fig leaves, are worthless as a covering. They tend to unravel over time, leaving us naked again. The only alternative is to go to God—to respond to His invitation of restoration—and allow Him to clothe us with Christ.

Those who live under shame tend to hide themselves by becoming the class clown, by making fun of themselves, or even by total denial. We also may cover ourselves by deflecting blame to someone else as Adam did when he said that it was the woman who tempted him.

Whatever the method, we spend our time focused on whatever is exposed. Shame is like a bad check that hasn't cleared your account. You dread its arrival at the bank and do everything you can to cover it before it does. Shame is the chronic feeling of insufficient means to cover a shortfall.

Bob was a brilliant man who taught high school math and economics. In our initial interview with Bob, it was very clear that he spent a lot of time trying to compensate and cover up for his imperfections. He was a very cerebral man who felt that he or anyone else could never do anything well enough. Though he had a strong faith, he was not sure how God really felt about him personally. Bob lived under the influence of shame.

During our ministry time, the Lord brought Bob to the memory of when he was very young and his family had visited friends in the East.

Before the end of their visit, Bob made some kind of silly remark to the family friends about their visit with them, which the friends laughed off as a feeble attempt at nine-year-old humor. His parents had a different opinion.

No sooner had they pulled out of the driveway than Bob's parents began to yell at him in the most demeaning way. They told him that he had embarrassed them in front of the family and said, "Shame on you!" Bob was crushed and melted into the floor of the backseat with his parents ending their tirade and giving him the silent treatment for the rest of the trip.

Fear and Separation

We already have spent an entire chapter on fear, but it is important to know, again, that the origin of fear is our separation from God. Adam said that he and Eve heard the sound of God's footsteps in the garden and became afraid. The source of the fear was their independence from God and the uncertainty of what might now happen to them.

When Adam and Eve chose to doubt God, they became separated from Him. They who were spiritual beings in close communion with God turned into two naked people in the midst of the garden. Shame and nakedness were felt for the first time anywhere. Only a little while before, when they were in communion with God, they were naked and not ashamed (see Gen. 2:25). But when they were separated from God and alone in their own frailty, shame set in. Shame is the focus on our sin and powerlessness to the exclusion of God's grace.

When the man and his wife heard the sound of God's footsteps, they ran away from instead of toward Him. We are so worried about the expectation of punishment that we miss the invitation of God to repent and be restored. Where God's intention for us is to be hidden *in* Him, shame makes us hide *from* God (see Col. 3:3).

When David fell into adultery with Bathsheba and murdered her husband, we have no information about his living close to the Lord. There are no psalms of praise and intimacy with God. He was separated by his sin and living in denial. One wonders how David conducted the affairs of state or his role as king/worshiper. Shame reduced David to living and ruling in his own strength, as it always does, because he was separated from the presence of God. It is important to know that this was not God's idea. God sent the prophet Nathan to lance the boil of David's sin that lived beneath the surface of his life.

Shame tells us that when we cross the line with God, His grace is not sufficient for us. David begged God for grace when his sin was uncovered. He said, "Be gracious to me, O God, according to Your lovingkindness" (Ps. 51:1a). When we live under shame, grace eludes us. We are fixed on our sin and not the Lord. Shame causes the weight of our sin to crush the life of God out of us. We hang our heads and can no longer look up to see God.

Covering Up

For those old enough to remember the days of Richard Nixon and the Watergate scandal, there was one phrase that got our late president and some of his associates in trouble. What they were guilty of was not the break-in itself, but the "cover-up" that followed. They attempted to hide the fact that something illegal and unethical had taken place. It was as bad as the actual crime because it attempted to sweep sin under the rug. The problem with sweeping things under the rug is that it tends to make lumpy carpets. The dirt is still there and will never be dealt with as long as we hide it.

Covering up is one of our carnal responses to sin. We may not have fig leaves readily available to us, but we still reach for some kind of disguise or covering. The cover-up may consist of doing some kind of works to try to hide our nakedness. Some of us get involved in ministry out of guilt rather than compassion, believing that we can somehow compensate for our failure by doing good. Again, some of us become perfectionists, hoping to cover our own inadequacies by holding everyone to an unattainable standard. The end result of inadequate works or self-perfection is that we never seem to be able to do enough or be good enough.

Those who live under the influence of shame see some kind of cosmic scales upon which God may consider the good things they do to counteract the bad things. But God is not an accountant and He has no scales. If He did, we could never hope to do enough good to outweigh the shortfalls we have. Instead, our approach to God is one of radical acceptance of His grace. The blood of Christ has tipped the scales in our favor. What can we add to that?

The problem with fig leaves is that they do not cover much and they always come apart. Whatever we do rather than face God with our sin and failure, whatever we do instead of throwing ourselves on His all-sufficient grace, will not get it done. The dirt will still be under the carpet. We will trip over it again.

Shame, fear, separation, and all the rest are not God's idea. There is much more to His love than we can hope to understand. The truth is that God is bent on cleaning up the mess—calling us back to intimacy with Him.

The Truth about Shame

When I was about six, our family lived on the Chestnut Ridge in western Pennsylvania. Somewhere along the line my mom got a new hurricane lamp with two floral globes trimmed in gold. She placed it on a table in a prominent place so as to give light over the whole room. She was, as I recall, very pleased with this new lamp.

One day, as little boys will do, especially twin boys, my brother and I were playing in the living room, throwing a ball back and forth. On one of the "forths," I threw the ball a little too hard and wide of my brother. Although *he* missed the ball, the lamp caught it. With that the top globe of the lamp fell off and broke on the floor. I was in shock. This was mom's new, prized lamp, and I had broken it. What should I do?!

Quickly, I took the broken part of the lamp and put it in the closet so that it would not be found. Then I packed whatever I could think of in a pillowcase and set off to forge a new life in the woods across the road. I knew that I had gone too far this time. I would be killed if I stayed around. So I went into the woods about 50 feet and watched for my parents to come home. (Our grandmother was watching us while they were away.)

After what seemed like days, but was in fact probably minutes, my grandmother called to me, telling me to come in the house. How did she know where I was? She must have been watching the whole time. She called, "It's time to come home, Tommy. Come back into the house." Of course, I could not ignore my grandmother, so I came the 50 feet back home.

My grandmother wasted no time asking me about the missing globe. I had to tell her what happened and where I had hidden it. She said something like, "You know better than to play like that in the house. It will be okay; we will get another globe." My sentence had been commuted. I was no longer the dead twin walking.

Shame had made me afraid and sent me into the woods. I'm sure I still go running into the woods sometimes. But the sound of "It's time to come home" will call me back, if I listen.

God Already Knows What We Are Trying to Hide

And there is no creature hidden from His sight, but all things are open and laid bare to the eyes of Him with whom we have to do (Hebrews 4:13).

The truth is that God was there to see the milk get knocked over. He was there and is still there waiting to bring you the truth about His love and grace in your life. Therefore, stop crying over spilled milk and let the Lord remove the shame that prevents you from fellowshipping with Him.

When I think of the grace of God, I go to that scene in the garden. Since there are no God-free zones in the universe, we know that God heard the sound of that apple core hit the ground. God knew exactly what had happened, and yet He came looking for the man anyway. I see and imagine the Lord Himself coming with a bucket and a mop, so to speak, to clean up the mess. God was sitting at the table when the milk was spilled! He saw the whole thing, yet His response was to come calling, "Adam, where are you?"

The reality of God's grace and heart toward cleaning up the mess was made clear when Jesus taught His disciples about servanthood. When they were in the upper room, Jesus grabbed a towel and a basin and showed them how to be like Himself. They were supposed to wash one another's feet and clean off the residual sin and the world from one another. The message is clear: No one should be kept from the table of God's grace.

God Calls Us to Himself

Then the Lord God called to the man, and said to him, "Where are you?" (Genesis 3:9)

"Where are you?" The question still resounds in our spiritual ears each time we fall into sin. God is not satisfied to leave us in the bushes. He calls to us and invites us to repentance and restoration in His presence. When man was created, he was naked and not ashamed because he was in relationship with God and dependent upon Him body, soul, and spirit. When we sin, when we blow it, God's response is to call us back into intimate fellowship. He calls out to us, "Where are you?"

Our problem is that we have a human and finite idea of the love of God. We are flawed and needy humans who seldom love without reason. We have a reason or rationale upon which to pin our affections for others—even our love of God. We love God more because of what He has done than for who He is.

John, "that disciple whom Jesus loved" (Jn. 21:7), tells us that we hide from God because we just don't understand the extravagant love of God.

> We have come to know and have believed the love which God has for us. God is love, and the one who abides in love abides in God, and God abides in him. By this, love is perfected with us, so that we may have confidence in the day of judgment; because as He is, so also are we in this world. There is no fear in love; but perfect love casts out fear, because fear involves punishment, and the one who fears is not perfected in love. We love, because He first loved us (1 John 4:16-19).

We can trust the love of God. His love is *perfect* love—a mature love, which means that it does not need anything else to be love. It is unconditional. God does not need us to do anything to enable Him to love us. He is not a man who needs His ego stroked or for us to give Him reason to love us.

God's love stems from His nature. "God is love" (1 Jn. 4:8b). My sin may control me sometimes, but it does not control God. God's only condition for loving me is for me to trust Him and stop trying to live in my own power for my own pleasure and glory. Paul tells us that "if you confess with your mouth Jesus as Lord, and believe in your heart that God raised Him from the dead, you will be saved; for with the heart a person believes, resulting in righteousness, and with the mouth he confesses, resulting in salvation" (Rom. 10:9-10).

God Is Not Separated from Us by Our Nakedness

> Who will separate us from the love of Christ? Will tribulation, or distress, or persecution, or famine, or nakedness, or peril, or sword? (Romans 8:35)

God knows us in our nakedness; He used to change our diapers. Make no mistake, God does not accept our sin—just as we would not approve of the sin and rebellion of our own kids. But God sees us as we see our children: as His own precious possessions. I don't look at, nor do I remember, the countless cups of milk my children have spilled. I only see my babies. So does God.

The truth is that none of us is perfect, none of us faithful. But God is perfect even when we are not perfect. Paul told Timothy that "if we are faithless, He remains faithful, for He cannot deny Himself" (2 Tim. 2:13). God cannot deny His own nature, which is one of sovereign love. He cannot help but to love us and invite us back into fellowship by the blood of Jesus Christ, dirty diapers and all.

Christ Took Our Nakedness to the Cross

> *Fixing our eyes on Jesus, the author and perfecter of faith, who for the joy set before Him endured the cross, despising the shame, and has sat down at the right hand of the throne of God* (Hebrews 12:2).

Jesus was naked and not ashamed because of His relationship with the Father. He took our nakedness upon Himself so that we could be clothed with His own righteousness. "For all of you who were baptized into Christ have clothed yourselves with Christ" (Gal. 3:27). No more fig leaves! God meets us in our guilt with grace, as the Psalm says: "You enlarge my steps under me, and my feet have not slipped" (Ps. 18:36). God has cleaned up the spill so that it will not stink up our relationship with Him. More than anything else, God wants us to be with Him. *No more crying over spilled milk!*

(See *Altars of the Heart Personal Ministry Guide*)

Getting the Picture

How does the picture of Adam and Eve resemble your life? Do you sometimes feel ashamed, guilty, embarrassed, foolish, like a failure, self-conscious, stupid, afraid, perfectionistic, and separated? Do you feel as though you can't do enough or that you just don't measure up? Have others called you a perfectionist?

Take a few minutes and write down ways that this picture looks like your life. Before you begin to write, acknowledge the presence and involvement of God through prayer. Do not proceed until you have bathed in prayer and His presence. Declare the intention of the Lord to bring you truth and healing and forbid any lies or interference from unclean spirits. Is there some spilled milk in your past?

Now, pray that the Lord would lead you to the source of those feelings. Ask Him to take you by the hand and lead you to a memory that feels like the recent event you described. Describe the memory picture in the frame below.

What are you feeling as you look at this memory frame? Why do you feel that way? What did you believe about that event? Now pray for the Lord to show you what is true.

I believed: _____

But the truth is: _____

Cleaning the House: Forgive, release as led of the Spirit.

What was true in the past is true in the present and will be God's promise to you in the future. Now revisit the present situation you cited at the beginning of this exercise. How do you see it now in light of what God has shown you?

The truth in the past was: _____

The truth in the present is: _____

God's promise to me for the future is: _____

Chapter Ten

LIVING ON THE LEDGE

Insecurity

The king said, "Is there not yet anyone of the house of Saul to whom I may show the kindness of God?" And Ziba said to the king, "There is still a son of Jonathan who is crippled in both feet." So the king said to him, "Where is he?" And Ziba said to the king, "Behold, he is in the house of Machir the son of Ammiel in Lo-debar." Then King David sent and brought him from the house of Machir the son of Ammiel, from Lo-debar (2 Samuel 9:3-5).

The Portrait of Insecurity

Here was a tall and handsome young man, born a prince over his people, the grandson of Saul, king of Israel: Mephibosheth. In other days, people would have bowed at his approach; they would have interrupted their lives just to catch a glimpse of this anointed son. He was the next in line of his grandfather Saul.

Mephibosheth was also the last in line of the house of Saul because both his grandfather and his father had been killed in battle years before. The shocking news of their deaths caused his nurse to drop him when he was still a small boy. The fall left him crippled, powerless for life. Then his own brother was murdered by those who tried to gain the favor of the new king.

Now the heir to the throne of Israel was hiding out on the backside of nowhere in Lo-debar, far from the security of the walls of Jerusalem. He lived in the guest house of a wealthy man, which was perched on a small ridge. From there he could see the approach of any threat.

It was the custom in those days for a new king to wipe out any remaining family members of the previous king who might pose a threat. Mephibosheth lived under the worry of a continuous threat from every corner. Anyone coming close to his secured ledge was a potential informant to the new king and therefore a great danger. He could trust no one. He was safe with no one.

This "should-have-been prince" now lived under constant fear of the servants of the king who now reigned over God's people. He and his family learned to sleep with one eye open—to live with a readiness to run at the slightest hint of danger. There was no rest, no place of repose where they could just enjoy life.

Day by day Mephibosheth sat by the window watching for a dust cloud that might betray the arrival of an informant. Now, perched on the ledge of his mountain sanctuary, he could see the dust of an approaching rider.

The Influence of Insecurity

The lie that inspires insecurity is "*I am not safe.*" Mephibosheth lived under the influence of what is best described as *insecurity*. He did not feel safe. Insecurity is the influence of the Perizzites, which comes from the Hebrew word *paratz*. It conveys the sense of being out in the open and unprotected. The simple meaning of the word is the best interpretation, and that is "someone who believes he lives in a place of vulnerability."

To be insecure is to live with a feeling of being unprotected, unsafe, powerless, or distracted. The insecure spend their time crunched up in a ball of self-protection and seldom get close to or trust anyone. They live on the ledge, watching for the next attack. The lie of insecurity is that everything is a threat.

Emotional Profile of Insecurity

Andrew was a bright young man in his late twenties who, to all appearances, had everything going for him. He was insightful and sensitive, but he also was one who lived with one eye open, so to speak. He was jittery and sometimes volatile in his marriage and even in his work.

Though he was very articulate, he found it hard to read or to stay focused on any task.

This bright and articulate young man and his wife came for ministry to get to the root of some of his fear and anxiety. During our initial time together and in the subsequent prayer time, several memories arose of a childhood that was, at best, unpredictable. Andrew had grown up in the rural South in the poverty of a single-parent household. He and his brothers were raised by his mother, who kept them away from others. The family lived in a secluded rural compound away from other people.

The children of this family, and especially Andrew, also lived under constant threat of severe and abusive punishment from their mother. The slightest thing of daily life would set her off into a rage that frequently included violence against her children. The mother would sometimes beat the children, chiefly Andrew, for no apparent reason other than her own anger and feelings of frustration. In fact, Andrew was regularly awakened during the night by his mother beating him with a broomstick or whatever else was handy. Needless to say, Andrew was never able to be at rest and slept every night with one eye open.

One particular memory that held much pain was one in which Andrew's mother sent him to find something in the pantry. Andrew looked for several minutes and could not find what his mother asked him for. Feelings of terror began to sweep over Andrew as he remembered the episode in vivid detail. He had the feeling that someone was about to beat him, to harm him in some way. (It reminded him of a similar feeling that he has at his current job, where he fills orders in a warehouse.) Andrew felt alone and very vulnerable as the scene of terror filled his mind. He believed that he was then, and was now, totally unprotected and out of control. He was living under the influence of insecurity.

When we asked the Lord to reveal His perspective on Andrew's remembered horror, the Lord spoke no words, but instead revealed Himself to Andrew as a surrounding presence. At first, Andrew was only vaguely aware of a presence around him in that pantry. But as the revelation unfolded, Andrew was aware of it in a more physical way in the form of a human hug. The truth was that Andrew was not alone and that the situation was in the hands of a loving and ever-present Father.

It was important to note that history did not change and that the abuse continued. But that wound no longer controlled Andrew, nor did the lie that no one was in control of the situation.

Andrew was a sort of modern-day Mephibosheth. He constantly felt unsafe, living on the ledge. Those who live on the ledge of insecurity usually experience feelings of anxiety, vulnerability, distrustfulness, and that everything is out of control. By definition, the strongest aspect of insecurity is the issue of control—or the lack of it.

Fear, Anxiety

Perhaps the most obvious effect of insecurity is fear or anxiety. Those who live under the influence of insecurity find themselves crunched up in a corner somewhere waiting for the other shoe to fall or for the next wave of attacks to hit their defenses.

We spoke in Chapter Six that the greatest fear is that of being alone, and there is a terrifying, empty aloneness that accompanies insecurity as well. Imagine Mephibosheth living on the side of a mountain, in terror that he might be discovered at any moment, that his life was no more secure than he alone could make it. When we live under insecurity, we believe that our life is in our own hands and we are terrified.

Threatened, Lack of Control

The Scriptures compare the insecure to a city whose walls are broken down. "Like a city that is broken into and without walls is a man who has no control over his spirit" (Prov. 25:28). It may be that we were raised in some kind of unsafe environment over which we had no control. We may have had an alcoholic or abusive parent like Andrew's mother or perhaps no parents at all, instead growing up on the streets. Some who live under insecurity may have been molested in some way and feel threatened when anyone invades their personal space. Whatever the source or reason, these people live outside the walls of protection.

The insecure believe that they are in life by themselves and that no one is watching out for them. They feel the need to control absolutely everything—from the way others see them to where they sit in the restaurant. They have to be in control of their environment and feel threatened when they are not. They are like Mephibosheth whom we picture living on top of a ridge so that he could see any approaching threat.

People who live in insecurity also feel the need to control others. They do so by manipulating people's emotions, as in using anger to make them afraid or pity to make them ashamed. They also may try to control others by sarcastic wit, which makes people reluctant to approach them. By whatever means, the insecure must be in control or they are out of control.

Those who feel threatened by insecurity—the ones whose walls have been torn down—will inevitably try to build other walls in order to feel safe and in control. These are walls of comfort. They will try to find comfort in things like food, sex, drugs, alcohol, new clothes, new cars or houses, or anything else over which they can exercise some kind of control. They build walls of addiction, manipulation, dissociation, indifference, or even compulsive behaviors. There are many strategies by which the unsafe build walls.

Books could be and have been written on each of the various results of feeling out of control. But the underlying reason for these behaviors is that people just don't feel safe. They are threatened by everything and everyone.

Volatile, Impulsive

There is a good reason for the little no-smoking sign that appears on gasoline pumps. The slightest spark from a cigarette could touch off a major explosion. The gas and particularly its fumes are very unstable or volatile. Those who live with insecure people know something about volatility. They know how the slightest spark can set off the most unreasonable responses. Things that seem to be nothing to us threaten the security of those who live on the ledge. As Proverbs 25:28 says, the insecure person has "no control over his spirit."

When it seems that our walls have been torn down and we are unprotected, we feel threatened by the slightest provocation and will put up a wall of anger that tells those around us, "Don't mess with me!" This keeps people out of range so they cannot threaten our safety zone.

This volatility is a different type of anger than what grows out of rejection. Rejection leads to a constant, seething kind of anger. The kind of anger that comes with insecurity, on the other hand, is a circumstantial, unpredictable, and intense kind of anger. It is what some might call a "short fuse."

We have seen this kind of anger from teens who feel unsafe because they have no boundaries. Children, especially teens, need some kind of boundaries to help them feel safe. When we remove structure, we also remove their security. The results will be explosive.

People who have suffered abuse of all kinds frequently feel trapped or frustrated by circumstances that remind them of the abuse they suffered.

For instance, we have seen both men and women who were sexually abused who cannot tolerate anyone coming into their space. They feel trapped, encroached upon. They respond to this trapped feeling like a frightened, cornered animal. They fight. When someone explodes in our faces, he or she is probably doing so because we are too close. We need to learn to respect personal perimeters and back off.

Volatile anger stems mostly from some feeling of frustration. It's like we are pushing against something heavy that refuses to budge no matter how hard we push. We get red in the face as we push and strain with all our might, but nothing moves. This is the look on the face of a baby who loses control of his bottle. It's that scrunched-up look that erupts into a red-faced tantrum. The problem is not that the baby is spoiled; the problem is that what he needs is out of his control.

Another response to insecurity is impulsiveness. Those who are insecure tend to live their lives according to whatever circumstances that arise. For example, they may buy things out of fear of missing a good deal or of looking foolish, rather than take the time to think about what makes sense for them. They are impulsive; they are compelled to react to the world rather than respond in what others may think are rational, sensible ways. In the end, people who act impulsively are not merely unwise; they are also unsafe.

When we are faced with what seems to be irrational anger, we need to get hold of our own security and then look beyond the explosion to where we will find a threatened child.

Defensive, Distrustful

The people on the ledge live there because it is defendable. People who live under the influence of insecurity feel that they must protect themselves from any threat, even verbal threats. They can never lose a point or give in to an argument, for to do so shatters their security. They must be right at all costs! They are perched on the edge of self-survival.

For them, a discussion is not a discussion; it's an assault on the fortress of self. Remember the story about two men who "discussed" what kind of cars they had? The angry man's reaction was not about a car; it was about feeling threatened by the slightest whiff of disagreement. The man who got the new car felt that his integrity was being attacked and had to defend himself. It seems irrational unless you are familiar with living on the ledge. There it makes perfect sense.

Another defense is simply not to trust anyone at all. Those who feel insecure find it very hard to form new relationships because relationships require trust. They cannot trust anyone. To trust is to let someone in, and that is just too much to risk. People must be kept out at all costs.

Powerless, Helpless

Mephibosheth was lame in both feet. In other words, he was completely powerless and helpless. He was immobilized in his disability. This is how the insecure see themselves: powerless, lame, helpless.

Many times they feel powerless in the origin of their insecurity. They may have been abused or terrorized at a young age, at a time when they could do nothing. Whenever their feelings of insecurity are triggered, they return to that same young age. My wife and I have found ourselves ministering to many children in grown-up bodies. Something became disconnected at the time of abuse and stopped growing.

Often I have found that those who live the loudest are the ones who feel the lamest. In other words, they compensate for their powerless immobility by directing everyone around them. They are the bullies who push kids around on the schoolyard but are themselves being beaten and terrorized at home. The only way they can achieve any kind of power is to terrorize someone else. The boss who yells at his employees is repeating the sound that still rings in his own ears. He is yelling out of his own powerlessness. He is less a bully than a beaten child trying to feel safe.

Solitary, Me against the World

Those who live on the ledge are usually there by themselves. The reason is obvious: Whom could they trust to be there with them? It's not that they don't want us there. It's that they can't risk having us there. Mephibosheth had to live a solitary life in order to avoid the threat of discovery by the king and possible death.

Those who live on the ledge live for themselves and by themselves. They feel like it's them against the world. Their lives spin in a centripetal pattern in which everything leads back to self.

Those on the ledge are constantly on the lookout for approaching threats. Although there are many indications of insecurity, ranging from denial to xenophobia, they all stem from the same belief that says, "I am not safe."

The Truth about Insecurity

Mephibosheth, the son of Jonathan the son of Saul, came to David and fell on his face and prostrated himself. And David said, "Mephibosheth." And he said, "Here is your servant!" David said to him, "Do not fear, for I will surely show kindness to you for the sake of your father Jonathan, and will restore to you all the land of your grandfather Saul; and you shall eat at my table regularly." Again he prostrated himself and said, "What is your servant, that you should regard a dead dog like me?" Then the king called Saul's servant Ziba and said to him, "All that belonged to Saul and to all his house I have given to your master's grandson. You and your sons and your servants shall cultivate the land for him, and you shall bring in the produce so that your master's grandson may have food; nevertheless Mephibosheth your master's grandson shall eat at my table regularly." Now Ziba had fifteen sons and twenty servants. Then Ziba said to the king, "According to all that my lord the king commands his servant so your servant will do." So Mephibosheth ate at David's table as one of the king's sons. Mephibosheth had a young son whose name was Mica. And all who lived in the house of Ziba were servants to Mephibosheth. So Mephibosheth lived in Jerusalem, for he ate at the king's table regularly. Now he was lame in both feet (2 Samuel 9:6-13).

The truth is that the King knows where we are, and He woos us off the ledge to His table. David, as a type of Christ, was not the typical usurper to the throne of Israel. He was placed there by God in the ultimate position of authority. Through a series of many battles, God gave him rest from his enemies (see 2 Sam. 7:1). So it was from this place of ultimate authority and total rest that David called and searched for someone to whom he could show kindness.

The Hebrew word for kindness here is *hesed*, which is the predisposition of God to demonstrate love for us. It is a bending, a stooping over to show us mercy. It is as though God's mercy is dripping over the railings of Heaven and falling on us. It is not something to which we are entitled; it is the unrestrained love of God that searches us out to bring us to Himself. Grace flows from the source of total authority.

There is a great picture of grace in the Book of Esther. When Esther entered into the king's chambers without his permission, he had the authority to kill her on the spot; instead, he extended his scepter to her. She touched the top of it and remained alive because the king gave her grace (see Esther 5:2). The king gave her what she could not get herself. She was powerless before his throne.

Grace flows from authority. Esther approached the king because she knew his heart. We can approach the King of Heaven the same way. He has called us to Himself, not to clobber us, but to love us. Grace, or kindness, is something we extend to someone who cannot obtain it for himself. We do it because we see that person's helplessness. It's like helping a turtle that is stuck on its back that would struggle and die without our intervention. When it comes to these inner healing issues, though, only God has the ability to turn our lives over again and set us right-side up on our feet.

There Is No Fear in God

We said before that "perfect love casts out fear" (1 Jn. 4:18). The first issue that the king dealt with was Mephibosheth's fear. David said, "Do not fear." We find our ultimate security in the One who is ultimately secure: God Himself. We can "set [our] mind on the things above, not on the things that are on earth [such as threats and things that make us insecure]. For [we] have died and [our] life is hidden with Christ in God" (Col. 3:2-3). We can look at God and know that He handles the threats. Nothing happens without God's knowing about it. God is our refuge and our stronghold. He is our hiding place. We are safe in His grace that flows from His total security.

> The Lord is my light and my salvation; whom shall I fear? The Lord is the defense of my life; whom shall I dread? When evil-doers came upon me to devour my flesh, my adversaries and my enemies, they stumbled and fell. Though a host encamp against me, my heart will not fear; though war arise against me, in spite of this I shall be confident. One thing I have asked from the Lord, that I shall seek: that I may dwell in the house of the Lord all the days of my life, to behold the beauty of the Lord and to meditate in His temple. For in the day of trouble He will conceal me in His tabernacle (Psalm 27:1-5a).

To be secure literally means to be without care. God is without care or concern. God is without fear. God is without rival. God is without want. When we are in God, we are these things as well. Even when the world around us seems threatening—indeed, when bad things happen—we are still safe in God and confident in His love for us.

We Live at God's Table

David said that Mephibosheth would eat at his table as his own son. In the same way, the King of the universe puts His own mantle of sonship upon us and we are secure in Him alone. Our ultimate security is in the love and grace of God Himself. The King will not leave us on the ledge. He brings us to His table.

Think for a minute about how Mephibosheth must have felt. Here was a man who was powerless and afraid, believing that he might be betrayed and discovered at any moment. He lived for years under the lie that he was in terrible danger and that his life was totally out of control. Now comes the messenger of the king, along with servants, to help Mephibosheth to a royal carriage. The king sent his own limousine to fetch this man to receive his grace.

Now Mephibosheth is before King David and throws himself at his feet, not knowing whether or not he will ever get up again. To his great astonishment, the king says, "Get up, and don't be afraid. I'm giving you everything your grandfather and father had and all the servants you need to carry you to the table. You're going to have breakfast, lunch, and dinner with me every day like one of my own sons."

Then, in what was the most telling moment, Mephibosheth was brought to the table at the hand of the king. He took his position there, his legs placed gently under the table. He was no longer lame, powerless, and defenseless. He was in the embrace of the king, his father's best friend.

The security we lost at someone's neglectful, disinterested, or abusive hand is now restored by the encompassing embrace of God as Father. We live securely within God's embrace—an embrace from which no one can remove us. Our lameness and insecurity are now under the King's table. The King relates to us solely on the basis of His own grace and provision. We are eternally secure at the table.

Now that we are secure in God, we can extend that grace to others. The very ones who abused us can be brought to the table themselves.

Why? Jesus told us to pray for those who abuse us (see Lk. 6:28). In so doing, we extend to them the same grace that brought *us* to the table. When another person is hungry—when they need what is at the table—they can sit next to us. The grace that we extend to them is the grace of the King, and we are free to give that grace because we live safely in His embrace.

The Lord Surrounds Us

Philip was a young man in his early thirties who was from the inner city. He and his wife were struggling because of an extramarital affair he had had. They found their way to our ministry center and began to pour out the pain of the experience. This seemed to be the end for them.

During the initial interview, it was obvious that Philip had been raised on the streets of the inner city. There was very little structure in his early life; he had no father at home. Philip struggled to feel settled and safe in his life. It was hard for him to relate to his wife in any spiritually intimate way. Philip couldn't get close to his wife or anyone else. He never felt safe with anyone.

When we prayed for the Lord to show him the source of his insecurity, he was reminded of when he was very young, sitting all alone in the living room of the apartment where his family lived. He felt alone abandoned...unprotected...insecure. He believed that he could not trust anyone and that he would have to be the one to control his world. When we prayed for the Lord to show him the truth, the Lord seemed to surround him as if to embrace him.

Philip wept—as, for perhaps the first time in his life, he felt safe and surrounded by love. Within minutes he was able to express his heartfelt, not legalistic, sorrow to his wife for the affair that had almost ended their marriage. He had looked for comfort and intimacy outside of his marriage. In that moment of truth, Philip was able to deal with his sin, and his wife was able to extend grace from a new perspective of grace. She had gotten inside Philip's heart and knew the circumstances that led to compromise. Healing had begun for both of them in the surrounding embrace of God's love.

The Scriptures are filled with promises of God's embracing presence for those who are secure in Him.

> *For it is You who blesses the righteous man, O Lord, You surround him with favor as with a shield* (Psalm 5:12).

Those who trust in the Lord are as Mount Zion, which cannot be moved but abides forever. As the mountains surround Jerusalem, so the Lord surrounds His people from this time forth and forever (Psalm 125:1-2).

... "Run, speak to that young man, saying, 'Jerusalem will be inhabited without walls because of the multitude of men and cattle within it. For I,' declares the Lord, 'will be a wall of fire around her, and I will be the glory in her midst'" (Zechariah 2:4-5).

O Lord, how my adversaries have increased! Many are rising up against me. Many are saying of my soul, "There is no deliverance for him in God." Selah. But You, O Lord, are a shield about me, my glory, and the One who lifts my head (Psalm 3:1-3).

Many are the sorrows of the wicked, but he who trusts in the Lord, lovingkindness shall surround him (Psalm 32:10).

The angel of the Lord encamps around those who fear Him, and rescues them (Psalm 34:7).

(See *Altars of the Heart Personal Ministry Guide*)

Getting the Picture

How does the picture of Mephibosheth's life on the ledge compare with your life? Are there times when you feel unsafe, threatened, out of control, volatile, powerless, defensive, distrustful, isolated, anxious, or like it's you against the world?

Describe a recent time when you felt the things described above. Before you begin to write, acknowledge the presence and involvement of God through prayer. Do not proceed until you have bathed in prayer and His presence. Declare the intention of the Lord to bring you truth and healing and forbid any lies or interference from unclean spirits.

Now, pray that the Lord would lead you to the source of those feelings. Ask Him to take you by the hand and lead you to a memory that feels like the recent event you described. This will be a root memory. Describe the memory picture in the frame below as you did with the recent event.

What are you feeling as you look at this memory picture? Why do you feel what you feel? What do you believe about that event? Now pray for the Lord to show you what is true.

I believed: _____

But the truth is: _____

Cleaning the House: Forgive, release as led of the Spirit.

What was true in the past is true in the present and will be God's promise to you in the future. Now revisit the present situation you cited at the beginning of this exercise. How do you see it now in light of what God has shown you?

The truth in the past was: _____

The truth in the present is: _____

God's promise to me for the future is: _____

Chapter Eleven

TORN SLEEVES

Defilement

The Portrait of Defilement

Tamar was a gentle rose coming to full bloom in the house of her father, the king. She had grown into a virtuous and beautiful young woman. She lived in the safety of the compartment allotted to her mother's children within the trusting enclave of her family. Tamar was, in a word, innocent.

As all the virtuous daughters of the king, Tamar wore a white garment with long sleeves to declare her purity and her relationship to her father the king. All who saw her knew that she was as clean and pure as her flowing white sleeves. The garment she wore was an outward indication of her inward condition and her unique and untouched value to her family and her father. She was whole and untouched, a precious treasure.

One day, word came from the king that she was to go to the house of Amnon, her half-brother, to prepare some bread to strengthen him in his illness. His illness appeared to be serious enough to cause the issue of a royal command to Tamar. Being an obedient daughter, she gathered makings for some bread to strengthen her brother's heart and left immediately.

As she arrived at the house, the other servants were ministering to the firstborn son of David. They were doing what they could to make him comfortable. Amnon was the heir to David's throne and therefore the object of much attention and indulgence—overindulgence.

As Tamar prepared bread for her brother, she took some in her hand and gave it to him, but he refused to eat it. Everyone left the room, and Amnon, pretending to be weak, said, "Please bring the bread into the bedroom." Of course, Tamar saw nothing wrong with going into the bedroom of her own half-brother. He was family—he was sickly—he was safe.

131

Tamar stretched out her hand to give her brother the bread she had made, but instead of taking her bread, he suddenly grabbed her. She was seized by a numbing horror. "Stop!" she declared. "This is wrong…you are my half-brother. How can this be? This is against the law of God. Stop!"

Now Amnon, who only moments before seemed too weak to eat, grabbed Tamar with the force of demonic lust. He threw her down and overpowered her innocent frailty, raping his own half-sister.

Now satisfied, Amnon's lust turned to disgust, and he pushed her away in anger. He had taken all that was precious from her and left her white sleeves as a mocking reminder of her lost wholeness.

"Throw this girl out of here," Amnon shouted to his servant. "She is of no further use to me."

"No, Amnon. Please don't do this. Everyone will think this was my fault. They saw me going into your bedroom. I will be ruined. Please don't—please don't."

But Amnon turned away from her, and his servant dragged Tamar out of the room, slamming the door behind her. She was left out in the dark—discarded like a dead animal along the road.

Now the white sleeves that denoted her purity only minutes earlier seemed to mock her broken and used condition. She tore them from her garment in mournful resignation. Picking up the dust from the ground, she threw it on her head, declaring her lost-ness. In those fleeting seconds, her life, with all its expectation and hope, was rubbed out, compromised. She was inconsolable in her grief.

When the king heard of all that happened he became angry, but he did nothing, which added fuel to Tamar's sense of loss. Her grief was public, but the sin against her was private. No one would ever know. No one would ever believe her.

Tamar stayed in the house of her brother Absalom, desolate and ruined. (See Second Samuel 13:6-20.)

The Influence of Defilement

The lie that inspires the influence of defilement is "*I am ruined for life.*" To defile something is to make it unclean. It is like taking a vessel filled with pure water and introducing one drop of sewage. Even if the filth was not visible to the naked eye, it would render the water unfit for human consumption. It is unclean, defiled. Whatever is defiled is dirty, bad, unfit.

Defilement is the *Hivite* influence. The word Hivite comes from the Hebrew word *havah*, which suggests natural or carnal life. It is the root from which Eve's name is taken. For the purpose of this book, we will say that the Hivites refer to a base or natural impulse—the natural life as opposed to the spiritual.

The references we find to the Hivites always seem to be associated with some kind of deception or perverse abuse. It was Shechem, the son of Hamor the Hivite, who lured Dinah to a place where he could rape and defile her (see Gen. 34:2). And it was the men of Gibeon, ethnically Hivites, who tricked the camp of Israel into making a covenant with them to avoid certain death (see Josh. 9:3-15). When we see the influence of the Hivites, we see defilement and deception.

The influence of defilement has several key components: abuse, an innocent or helpless victim, an overpowering abuser, and disregard for the victim. All of these leave the victim—the defiled—with a sense that he or she is ruined for life. Many times, in fact most of the time in our experience, the abuser is close to the victim and should have been trustworthy, so there is also a strong sense of betrayal.

Defilement does not happen exclusively because of sexual assault of some kind. The ruin of defilement comes as the result of betrayed innocence.

My father was a good and decent man who worked for the same company for 35 years. He was a dedicated employee, a company man. He gave his best year after year and became the head of his department. He was there to guard the office when the labor union went on strike. He worked Saturdays on special projects when the load was heavy. He picked up his family and moved hundreds of miles away when the company needed him to. He was a true company man. When he reached the age of 55, he could see that he was headed for the homestretch toward retirement. Given his long and faithful service to the company, he expected to work another 15 years or so and then retire on the full pension he had worked so long to accrue. It didn't quite work out that way.

One day as he was working at his desk, two men walked into his office wearing polite but impersonal smiles. Out of the blue they informed him that he and the senior people in his department were going to be phased out and retired early, that the company was going in another direction with younger men. With a pat on the back they told him he would be given a reduced pension and that it was nothing personal.

He was shipwrecked. It was the first time I heard my dad cry. Dad was left feeling betrayed by the very people he had served so well for many years. The ones who promised to take care of him were the very ones to take advantage of him in his innocent devotion to them. He crumbled into a realm of insecurity and desperate depression. All that seemed solid and stable to him was destroyed. He believed that at his age he would never find work again. He was an innocent victim abused by the overwhelming power of people who discarded him when they were finished with him. He was defiled in every sense of the word.

Defilement and the ways to avoid it were a big part of the Old Testament laws. Anything that was defiled was not allowed to be in God's presence. There were voluminous rules to keep things undefiled and even more as to how they might be cleansed. The Book of Leviticus is filled with such rules to stay clean. People who had defiling diseases like leprosy were separated out as unclean to prevent them from touching (thus defiling) anyone else. Anything that would, or could not, be cleansed of defilement was thrown out of the camp so as not to contaminate anyone or anything else.

When people are used for someone else's personal gain or pleasure without regard for their own good, it is an abnormal use, or an "ab-use." When people are abused and discarded, they live under the influence of defilement. Tamar was "ab-used" by her half-brother, Amnon, then thrown out in the cold. She was no longer pure in her own estimation. She was unfit for normal human relationships. She was left a desolate victim living in her brother Absalom's house, her hopes of a productive life with marriage and children dashed.

The influence of defilement leaves an imprint on the emotions of the defiled. It is a unique combination of insecurity, hopelessness, and shame.

Emotional Profile of Defilement

Betrayed, Confused

One of the key elements of defilement is that of betrayal. To be betrayed is to be abused by someone we otherwise know and trust. It may be parents, a pastor, a teacher, or a sibling. That is the factor that makes it most damaging. Not only is something precious taken from the abused, but their trust is destroyed at the same time, leaving them in a confused state.

My wife and I have ministered to people who have been abused by all the categories above. One instance of abuse that was particularly damaging happened at the hands of a church deacon. The abuse was one of talking in suggestive and very inappropriate ways to a teenage girl, as well as inappropriate touching, which left the young girl confused. The betrayal was so unconscionable that the girl blotted it from her memory for more than 20 years until it surfaced during a ministry session.

Perhaps the worst part of this type of betrayal is that no one believes the victim when the abuse is reported. I recall a case in which abuse happened to a young girl by a pastor who was a friend of the family. When the girl reported it to her parents, she was the one who got punished for saying such a thing. All of this leaves the victim feeling as though there is nowhere to go—no one to protect her who will understand. The result is that the anger and hurt are pushed below the surface, just waiting to erupt at a future time. And it will erupt.

Violated, Damaged

Tamar begged her brother not to violate her. To be violated is to be broken into some way; it's when someone crosses a line that should never be crossed. Violation occurs when clearly posted signs are ignored and the perpetrator disregards the law—like someone who chooses to break the speed limit or who doesn't fully halt at a stop sign. The main feeling of violation is one of someone forcing his way to a forbidden place. Such was the case with Amnon, who clearly thumbed his nose at the law of God and the welfare of his half-sister.

When we have been violated, we feel that nothing and no one is safe. Once someone has jumped over the fence, it is pretty hard to feel anything but shocked and unprotected. The abused lose the sense of safety; they now know that the lines of respect and proper behaviors are only lines that someone else may choose to ignore. The fence is broken down and flattened by the disregarding lust of another person.

I recall a recent session in which a young woman had been so abused that she couldn't close her eyes to pray. To close her eyes would require trusting that I would not harm her in some way. She had been violated by two family members from a young age. To add to the trauma, her own father, who enjoyed a prominent position in the community, did not believe her story. Instead he punished her, making her feel doubly unsafe. He did not want the tales of abuse to get out and considered his reputation to be more important than her safety. So the abuse continued.

Disgraced, Degraded

To feel disgraced is to believe that there is no grace for us. This particular word carries the sense of foolishness or degradation. To be degraded or disgraced is to feel that we somehow have descended to a lower rung on the ladder, that we are no longer precious or valuable. We feel that we have no rights.

Sometimes the feelings of degradation are so complete that the victim steps down to that lower rung and begins to act out his or her degradation. Many of those to whom we minister who lived in lifestyles of sexual perversion or drug abuse can trace their struggles back to the time when they were abused themselves. They reasoned that since they were damaged goods, they might as well live that way. They see themselves as lesser people.

Shameful, Dirty

Defilement leaves people with a feeling of being dirty or shameful in some way. Even though they are the ones who have been defiled, they somehow blame themselves. Tamar was concerned that her brother's turning her out would make it look as though she was the guilty party. She said, "Sending me away is greater than the other that you have done to me!" (2 Sam. 13:16b). She thought that somehow she would be seen as the guilty party.

Those who have been abused, particularly sexually, believe that they had something to do with the offense against them or that they could have prevented it somehow. Perhaps they believed themselves to be foolish or stupid. My wife and I have ministered to women who were raped who said, "It was my fault. I should have known better than to be in that place or with that person." Whatever the specific words they use, they somehow believe that the defilement reflects guilt and blame on them.

When we ministered to the young woman who couldn't close her eyes because of fear, a memory surfaced of that cruel violation. As we looked at a memory filled with abuse, the young girl shuddered and hyperventilated in terror. Her security was compromised by the very ones who should have made her feel safe. It was so horrible that I asked her for no details.

The striking thing about the memory was that even though she was the one being abused, she said that she was bad, that she was dirty.

Tamar said, in effect, "How will I get rid of this shame that is on me?" (see 2 Sam. 13:13) As we said in an earlier chapter, shame becomes like a defiling mud that sticks to us, not allowing us to get close to God or anyone else. This is even more so with the person who feels defiled. The abuse perpetrated against Tamar—the abnormal use of her body by her own half-brother—would cling to her for the rest of her life with no way of getting free of it.

Ruined, Spoiled Goods

In perhaps the most telling statement of all, the biblical text tells us that Tamar was desolate in her brother Absalom's house. To be desolate is to be like a howling wasteland, like a ghost town being reclaimed by the desert as in the Old West. The songs that were once sung are heard no longer; the activity and bustle of life are no longer in evidence. We could easily replace the word *desolate* with *ruin*, which evokes a picture of the ancient dilapidated cities with walls crumbling and no hope of future life. This is the feeling of many under the influence of defilement.

When someone has been abused and lives under the influence of defilement, the motion of their lives comes to a screeching halt. They believe themselves to be spoiled just as Tamar did, who tore the sleeves off of her garment in a symbolic motion of the end of her innocence and life as she hoped it might be. All that seemed to be good and precious had gone bad like a carton of milk left out of the refrigerator.

The defiled live in a continuous state of mourning. Tamar threw ashes on herself as though they were the ashes of incinerated hope, and she walked about with her hand on her head bewailing her condition. Like Tamar, people who are under the influence of defilement live as though they are at their own funerals, gazing at pictures of their days of innocence. For them life is over and they can't see how the ruins of their lives can ever be inhabited again.

I recall again how my own father who, when he was forcibly retired in favor of younger men, felt as though he would never work again, that he would never live another purposeful day. He believed, like Tamar did, that his life was spoiled, that it had gone bad and would never again amount to anything. God, however, had other plans.

These and other feelings crop up to rob the defiled of intimacy with God. But God, who is faithful and compassionate, invites us back into His presence to heal our wounds and restore us.

The Truth about Defilement

During ministry, the young woman who had been molested by family members came to a place of terror on confronting the memory picture. It was so vivid and real to her, it was as though it might happen to her again. She said, "I was bad"; she said that it was her fault. But when we asked the Lord to show her the truth—what He believed about her and the abuse—He simply said, "I love you." It was all she needed to hear. It was proof that she was still precious and valuable. With that the hyperventilation and trembling stopped, as if turned off by a switch.

Once the trembling stopped, the Lord said, "This was not your fault; you are not bad."

With that the guilt and slime of shame was lifted off of her. She was able to hear what the Lord said, and she was able to close her eyes to receive a blessing and the truth, which is our usual conclusion to the ministry session.

The Truth Is That It Is Not Your Fault

Note that we could not change history; she had been abused. But now she saw that the Lord had not left her alone. She was safe in His love. She found Someone to trust. With that, her defensiveness and distrust began to evaporate. She was safe in the embrace of God. The Torah is clear on whose sin the abuse is:

> But if in the field the man finds the girl who is engaged, and the man forces her and lies with her, then only the man who lies with her shall die. But you shall do nothing to the girl; there is no sin in the girl worthy of death, for just as a man rises against his neighbor and murders him, so is this case (Deuteronomy 22:25-26).

The truth is that you were the one sinned against. You did not participate of your own free will. There was probably little or nothing you could do to stop the attack. You trusted someone else who took advantage of that trust to satisfy his own need without regarding yours. The thought never occurred to Tamar that her own half-brother would rape her. She went into his room to minister to him and nothing else. It is perhaps true that some unwise behavior allowed the abuse to occur, but she was in no way to blame for the sin of another person.

God Was with You

The most frequent opposition to healing in this scenario is the notion that God could not possibly have been there when we were abused. This is because we believe either that the sin against us was too great or that somehow God just abandoned us to our abuser. Many times people who were abused said there was no way that the Lord could have been there. If He loved them, why did He allow it to happen? The truth is, however, that God was there even in that place and that He never stopped loving them for a moment.

Time after time those to whom the Lord is ministering healing have sensed the presence of God around them. God had not abandoned them to the abuser. He was there, and because God is not bound by time or dimension as we are, God would see the very day of their healing even as they were being abused. The truth is that people do bad things because they choose to; they have free will. But those bad things are never God's idea. God always leads us back to His embrace and healing, even from the greatest wounding.

Life Is Not Over

Although the following Scriptures apply to the nation of Israel, they also point to God's predisposition to heal and restore those who are living ruined lives. God desires to bring us back to Himself and into fruitful lives. Our lives are not over because of the sin of another person. As God heals us, we find a new life anchored in His healing presence and compassion. God will restore us to all that we ever were intended to be in Him.

> *Also I will restore the captivity of My people Israel, and they will rebuild the ruined cities and live in them; they will also plant vineyards and drink their wine, and make gardens and eat their fruit* (Amos 9:14).

> *For the Lord will restore the splendor of Jacob like the splendor of Israel, even though devastators have devastated them and destroyed their vine branches* (Nahum 2:2).

(See *Altars of the Heart Personal Ministry Guide*)

Getting the Picture

How does the picture of Tamar's experience compare with yours? When do you feel betrayed, confused, violated, damaged, shameful, dirty, ruined, spoiled, unclean, useless, or anything similar to these emotions? Before you begin to write, acknowledge the presence and involvement of God through prayer. Do not proceed until you have bathed in prayer and His presence. Declare the intention of the Lord to bring you truth and healing and forbid any lies or interference from unclean spirits.

Can you describe a recent time when you felt the things described above? Write a brief description in the picture frame.

Describe what you were feeling in that recent event.

Now, pray that the Lord would lead you to the source of those feelings. Ask Him to take you by the hand and lead you to a memory that feels like the recent event you described. Describe the memory picture in the frame below as you did with the recent event. (Note that there may be more than one. Try to find the oldest memory.)

What are you feeling as you look at this memory frame? Why do you feel that way? What did you believe about that event? Now pray for the Lord to show you what is true.

I believed: _____

But the truth is: _____

Cleaning the House: Forgive, release as led of the Spirit.

What was true in the past is true in the present and will be God's promise to you in the future. Now revisit the present situation you cited at the beginning of this exercise. How do you see it now in light of what God has shown you?

The truth in the past was: _____

The truth in the present is: _____

God's promise to me for the future is: _____

Chapter Twelve

STARING INTO EMPTINESS

Hopelessness

But Mary was standing outside the tomb weeping; and so, as she wept, she stooped and looked into the tomb; and she saw two angels in white sitting, one at the head and one at the feet, where the body of Jesus had been lying. And they said to her, "Woman, why are you weeping?" She said to them, "Because they have taken away my Lord, and I do not know where they have laid Him" (John 20:11-13).

The Portrait of Hopelessness

She just couldn't sleep. She tossed and turned all night long thinking, wondering, weeping. Her Lord had delivered her from seven devils; He could open up the Word of God to her like none other. She had seen Him do many miracles—countless wonders among the desperate and poor. But the image that remained in her heart was that of His broken body as it hung from the rough wooden emblem of shame—a body that was now as cold and lifeless as the rock-hewn tomb to which it had been carried. Now what would become of her life? What kind of future could there be for a healed hooker? She had burned all her bridges to follow this Man. It was dark.

As the night wore on in a monotonous, stinging barrenness, the oil in the little clay lamp on the wall was running out. In her pain she had not bothered to refill it. As the light flickered with the last drop of oil, Mary looked outside the window of her little house and saw that the sky had gone from black to an indigo blue as dawn and the end of her troubled sleep were at hand.

The woman called the Magdalene arose from her bed, which had not given sleep to her the whole night before, her eyes puffy and tired from her weeping. Though she respected the Sabbath, it had been more like a sentence than a time of rest. She could wait no longer to visit the tomb of her Lord. So Mary set out from her house in the predawn hour with a bundle of spices to finish the preparation of the body of Jesus.

Now, as she drew near to the tomb in the dim of predawn, she was astonished to see that the large stone in front of the tomb had already been rolled away. Mary rushed to the mouth of the tomb carved into the rocky hillside and stooped over to see inside. As she looked in, two angels in the form of young men sat there, one at the head and the other at the foot of where the body of Jesus had lain. Her mourning heart was prepared to see the body of her Lord, but it was not there.

Her restless and tired body now became alive with shock and conjecture. What had they done with the body of her crucified Lord? Wasn't it enough that they had whipped and mutilated Him while He was alive? Who would have taken away His lifeless body? The two angels on the empty slab looked into Mary's face with a restful calm and asked, "Why are you weeping?"

What a cruel and thoughtless question. "Someone has taken away my Lord," she answered.

Mary was left stooped over and weeping at the empty tomb. All that she expected—all she had ever hoped in the great Man she followed—came to a pointless end in a cold and empty hole in the rock. She was staring into emptiness—the picture of hopelessness.

The Influence of Hopelessness

The lie that inspires hopelessness is "*I will never….*" You can fill in the rest of the sentence. For us, as with Mary, hope is the thing that keeps us moving forward toward some positive expectation. We hope that our children find good mates and settle down. We hope that the doctor's diagnosis is favorable. We hope that the stock market rises and carries our 401k plan with it. Our hope in any situation is for a positive outcome according to our understanding.

I saved my own story for this chapter since hopelessness and depression are my own issues. I have had seasons of staring into emptiness when nothing made sense and my life seemed to come to a senseless and confusing halt.

I spent most of my thirties building a retail music company. My wife and I bought a small company in the little town of Chambersburg,

Pennsylvania, in 1983, investing all of our savings. The business grew well and in a few years was doing many times the sale volume that it did before we purchased it. Things seemed to be going well, and I could begin to see the flicker of a prosperous future just over the horizon.

Both Carol and I grew in our faith during those years, and that faith spilled over into the business. We paid our tithes and enjoyed intercession and a fair amount of ministry in the store. Things seemed to be moving along. By and large we were hopeful of a bright and secure future. But all was not well in musicland.

Eventually the bottom fell out of the music market, at least in the areas where we had invested our efforts. Within a couple years' time our growing business went south and we were broke. Finally, we went into bankruptcy and spent a year working for another dealer while at the same time trying to liquidate our business so as to keep our default to a minimum. We were able to pay off most of our debt and reorganize the rest, but we were devastated. All seemed bleak—and on top of it all, I was now 40. The question on my mind then was, Who would want a 40-year-old failure like me? How would I make a living? My vision of the future barely reflected the limited revelation of God's plan that I did have.

That, however, was not the end of anything; it was only the beginning. After a few months my life totally changed. True, I was out of the music business that until then had been my life, but now I was in the arena of Christian publishing and headed toward full-time ministry. You see, while in the music business, I had taken a few courses at a nearby Bible college and studied Hebrew for a couple years with a local rabbi who became a close friend. That directed this new stage in my life, and it could not have been more different. I began to see that neither God's plan nor His love for me had ceased when we closed our store in failure. It was not the end; it was only the beginning. God had been with me the whole time and is with me now as I write these words.

Hoping and seeing go together, but it is a seeing with the heart rather than with the eyes. Maybe we could call it "vision." The Bible tells us that we hope for what we do not see. If we saw it, we wouldn't have to hope for it; it would already be in our hands. (See Romans 8:24-25.) We would not hope for a raise in salary that we already had. But we might hope—we might dare to speculate on what we would do with that extra money if it was to come to us. Whatever we see ourselves doing with that extra money is what we hope for.

Hopelessness is the influence of the Jebusites, whose name may be interpreted as downtrodden or beaten down. When I think of the Jebusites, I see a people who excelled in dashing hopes and expectation. It was the Jebusites in Second Samuel 5 who controlled the citadel of Jerusalem. As King David moved toward establishing his reign on Mount Zion, it was the Jebusites who told him he didn't have a prayer of doing so. They put their blind and lame on the walls to taunt him, saying, "You will never get in here." The words *hopeless* and *trampled* seem to fit well together.

Never is the operative word of hopelessness. We see only obstacles and no way to get around them. Hopelessness is taking the visible evidence, comparing it to what we know, and determining that we will never get there...we will never make it...never...never...never. Hopelessness is the belief that something is impossible, given our understanding of reality. For example, we look at our checkbook and then the bills, and we determine that—based upon our understanding and resources—there is no hope of paying all of them.

The universal response to hopelessness is to simply quit. It is as though we are in a rowboat moving into a fog. When we can no longer see ahead, we just give up and stop rowing. We sit in the fog and wait for something bad to happen. When we can't see or understand, we don't move ahead.

Hopelessness kills our desire for life. Many older people die for lack of vision and hope. They see nothing further they can do and despair of any further purpose in their lives. "Where there is no vision [no hope], the people perish" (Prov. 29:18a KJV). There is a blight on the senior population of our nation because we have been taught a retirement mentality. We not only retire from a job; we also retire from life and hope.

We hope for what we see. When we can no longer see, we no longer hope. We become hopeless.

Emotional Profile of Hopelessness

There are several emotions that flow out of hopelessness. When we are under the influence of hopelessness we feel...

Cursed, Doomed

"This just isn't going to go my way...Things will never work out...Nothing will ever change...Here we go again...." These are the words and feelings of the hopeless.

To feel cursed is to feel as though there is a heavy and inescapable weight of impending doom assigned to our lives, as though we are the children of a lesser God. We've seen this many times in the lives of those who have come out of prison—or even in their children, who believe that it is their lot in life to follow their parents to prison.

Once when I was visiting the warden of the local county jail, he told me that the children of those in prison were seven times more likely to find themselves there in the future. I'm not sure where he got his statistics, but he could rattle off several instances of multiple generations in his own prison. What's worse is that the children of the inmates in his prison naturally expected to be there; it became part of the culture of their futures. Such is the influence of hopelessness.

Hope-less-ness is exactly that: living under the curse of a lesser hope. I think of Mary Magdalene who was delivered from seven devils. (By the way, that is a Bible way of saying that she was completely bound by the enemy.) Imagine the emotion and the self-talk that flooded her heart as she looked into the empty tomb. "Here we go again...I was never really free...I have no where else to go." It was a feeling that left her stooped over and weeping at an empty tomb.

Defeated

When we live under the influence of hopelessness, we live with the white flag of surrender raised over us. We have surely been defeated and the only thing left for us to do is to work out the terms of unconditional surrender to a lesser life and a lesser hope. As a result, we walk around with heads hung as low as our expectations.

When we give in to feelings of defeat, we play into the enemy's hands. He wants us to believe that we have been beaten, that he is stronger. David talks about the taunts of his enemies over his own life and reign:

A Psalm of David, when he fled from Absalom his son. O Lord, how my adversaries have increased! Many are rising up

*against me. Many are saying of my soul, "There is no deliver-
ance for him in God"* (Psalm 3:1-2).

It is not hard to feel defeated when the casualties begin to pile up
around us. When we have tried our hardest and still get nothing better
than C's on our report card; when we have given it all we've got and our
spouse still chooses adultery—we feel as though the battle is over and all
hope is lost. At that point our flag is fallen and the enemy has his way
with us. However, to be sure, it is not the end of the story!

Indifferent, Resigned

Many who cannot see hope for tomorrow simply stop looking for it.
They stay within the confines of their limited perspectives. There is a
feeling that life exceeds their grasp, that every time their hand is on the
doorknob of opportunity it will not turn. The result is that sooner or later
they just stop reaching and quit.

Those who have lived under hopelessness resign in every sense of
the word. They quit. They think that there is no reason to go on since they
will fail anyway. Their hope becomes calloused and they become indif-
ferent; they no longer care. Again, they are the image of Mary weeping
at an empty tomb. A hole in the ground has little hope or motivation to
move us forward. Therefore, we just stop moving.

Pessimistic, Negative

Once we have stopped moving, we begin to see everything as futile.
We become missionaries of hopelessness and see the world in a negative
light. Nothing will ever work out; nothing will ever be the same again.
We become like Eeyore, the little stuffed donkey in the Winnie the Pooh
stories. For him, life was the sound of the other shoe falling. There was
no use looking forward to anything because life just doesn't work out and
that's the way it is.

There is a supreme irony in the scene of Mary before the empty
tomb. The very thing that should have encouraged her—an empty tomb—
was the thing that made her feel hopeless. If she had had a proper revelation of what Jesus always said He was going to do, she would have
rejoiced at the fact that He had arisen. But Mary looked at the empty tomb
with human understanding and, instead of jumping for joy, she was sad.

Pessimism and negativity are the result of our woefully deficient
human understanding. We take what we have learned in the past—our

own experience and understanding—and we predict the future. To Mary an empty tomb meant a missing body rather than a resurrected Lord. She was left with no thought that Jesus was more than she thought He was. Her view of the future and her hope of ever seeing Jesus again was dashed. Her best hope now was to find her dead Rabbi and give His body a decent burial. New revelation was standing right behind her all the time. She just didn't recognize it. Neither do we when we are living under the influence of hopelessness.

Disappointed, Empty

Sometimes we spend our time dreaming and expecting things that do not happen. We might say that we *appoint* something to happen. Then, when it doesn't, we become dis-appointed from that expectation. We are separated from our vision. Perhaps a woman dreams all of her life of having and holding her own baby. She sees herself nursing and loving a tiny gift of precious life. Then the doctor finds an abnormality that makes it difficult for her to have children. What she has dreamed of all her life may never happen as she has seen it. All that she has hoped for may never come to fruition. She becomes as Mary was, staring into emptiness. The thing entombed was her hope, which is now dead in its absence.

I can recall many cases where spouses have wrapped their lives around their mates, taking their entire significance from that marriage—only to have that spouse die or leave. That absence creates a giant, life-sucking vacuum that draws everything into it. These spouses try to fill the emptiness with activity. They try to fill it with denial. But in the end they are left with a hole that can never be filled. To be sure, the greatest disappointment may be caused because their expectations were too high. They may have been too consumed with the marriage and less grounded in God. Whatever the reason, the hopeless are left feeling grieved, disappointed, and empty.

Depressed

Perhaps the most pronounced emotion under the influence of hopelessness is depression. Depression is the feeling that we are standing on the precipice of a bottomless pit and cannot seem to find the energy to move back from the edge. There seems to be no way out and nowhere to go but over the edge. The only vision we have is of ourselves falling through the empty blackness, waiting for the inevitable destruction.

I must admit that I have felt defeated many times in ministry. There are those to whom we don't seem to be able to bring healing. The ones we love the most—the ones we invest the most in—are sometimes the most difficult to minister to. Perhaps this is why the Lord grants us an extra measure of love for them.

Many times I have felt as though I am staring into a deep, dark, and empty hole whose dimensions threaten to swallow up my life and ministry. I cannot see how anything I have done or could ever do might bring healing to severely abused or disturbed people. I love them, but in that love I feel helpless and lost. In a word, I am depressed.

Depression is a common problem in our society today with many people taking antidepressant drugs. It seems that every other person we meet is on Prozac. Life for these people has gotten so complicated, so black, that they have lost all vision in the ever-increasing tangles of worry, children, career, world tensions, retirement plans, and all the rest. They are caught on the horns of hopelessness with little thought of anything ever working out.

All of these—doom, defeat, indifference, resignation, pessimism, emptiness, depression, and disappointment—are the fruit of hopelessness. They are formidable obstacles to moving forward into the abundance of God. All of them are the product of limited revelation of the Person and work of Jesus Christ. But there is a greater revelation coming that leads us to the truth about hope.

The Truth about Hopelessness

When she had said this, **she turned around and saw Jesus standing there, and did not know that it was Jesus.** *Jesus said to her,* **"Woman, why are you weeping? Whom are you seeking?"** *Supposing Him to be the gardener, she said to Him, "Sir, if you have carried Him away, tell me where you have laid Him, and I will take Him away."* **Jesus said to her, "Mary!" She turned and said to Him in Hebrew, "Rabboni!"** *(which means, Teacher). Jesus said to her, "Stop clinging to Me, for I have not yet ascended to the Father; but go to My brethren and say to them, 'I ascend to My Father and your Father, and My God and your God.'" Mary Magdalene came, announcing to the disciples,*

"I have seen the Lord," and that He had said these things to her (John 20:14-18).

As Mary was stooped over and weeping into the emptiness, she became aware of a presence at her back. Turning around momentarily from her dark focus, she saw what appeared to be the gardener, the one in charge of the cemetery. No sooner had His appearing interrupted her grief than He asked her the same thoughtless question the angels had: "Why are you weeping?", but then He added, "Whom are you seeking?"

In her tortured disappointment she thought that perhaps He had carried the body of her Lord away. After all, it was a borrowed tomb. Maybe the owner wanted it back. She said to the gardener, "Please tell me where You have put His body. I'll carry Him to another tomb."

Just then, as she was turning her attention back to the emptiness, the figure behind her, whose presence she had felt, spoke one word. "Mary!" He spoke as if to awaken her from the slumber of inadequate revelation. "Mary!" She was awakened as from a dead sleep by a voice that resonated against her deepest hope. Her mind was overwhelmed by her thrilled heart. Something like scales fell from her eyes as she recognized the identity of the presence that had been behind her. Now, fully and finally turned around, she said, "My Master!"

Jesus had gone from Lord to her LORD.

As she spoke these words, she grabbed onto the hem of His garment, but the risen Lord said, "Don't hang onto Me, or onto who you think I am. Instead, go and tell the others who have not seen Me who I really am."

With that Mary ran to the others who loved Jesus and said, "I have really seen the LORD."

Our Hope Is Alive

In her grief at the empty tomb, Mary missed something that we might observe 2,000 years later. There were two angels sitting at the head and foot of the place where the body of Jesus had been laid. They were "sitting." Why? Because there was nothing else to be done. Everything was under control. They were not concerned as she was. For a moment, those angels had a greater revelation of Jesus, who was more than a dead itinerant rabbi. He was the Lord of life, the eternal One, the Creator. He was alive! "Blessed be the God and Father of our Lord Jesus Christ, who according to His great mercy has caused us to be *born again to a living hope* through the resurrection of Jesus Christ from the dead" (1 Pet. 1:3).

We humans tend to see our lives in a static plan of action and reaction, of sequence and consequence. "For we know in part and we prophesy in part" (1 Cor. 13:9). The reality is that while things may seem hopeless according to our understanding, they are very much intact in God's view. The problem is that we just do not see it.

Get this picture. While Mary was standing stooped over, staring into the emptiness, Jesus was standing right behind her all the time. While she was seeing the end of her hope and vision, the presence of God was practically breathing down her neck. She did not see Him at first because of her disappointed expectations. But there He was, alive and inviting her to see Him.

What was required in order for Mary to see her living hope was that she turn around. To turn around from a Hebrew perspective is to repent, from the word *shuv*. This means that we move in a new direction. How many times are we staring into emptiness when all the time the Lord is standing behind us? The Lord Himself is right there speaking our name and rousing us from our *focus on circumstances*. All we have to do is to turn around to see Him.

Our hope is based more on what we can't see than on what we can see. "For in hope we have been saved, but hope that is seen is not hope; for who hopes for what he already sees? But if we hope for what we do not see, with perseverance we wait eagerly for it" (Rom. 8:24-25).

When we are suffocating under the influence of hopelessness, we need to ask God to enable us to see Him. So often we consider His presence for a moment, then turn back to the emptiness. That is why our Christian lives seem to jerk from one crisis to the next—or from one miracle to the next.

As we consistently see the presence of the living Christ, we find hope that won't disappear with the next overdraft notice from the bank. We find hope that won't fade away with our looks (for those of us who have looks, that is). We will approach even the most hopeless situation with eagerness to see the presence of God revealed. We have a living hope.

Our Hope Is in a Person

Jesus not only asked Mary, "Why are you weeping?" but also "Whom are you seeking?" Mary came to the tomb seeking an "it," not a "whom." She came expecting to find a body, a deceased shell of a great teacher and miracle worker.

There is a connection between what we seek—what we are focused on—and what we feel. What we feel comes from what we believe or trust. Therefore, Mary must have believed that Jesus was a great Rabbi, a compassionate healer, a kindly and personable friend, but she did not believe Him to be the Lord. Her hope ended at the mouth of the tomb.

In reality, Mary, the one who loved and followed Jesus so closely, had no greater revelation and hope than did the Pharisees and priests who crucified Him. They asked that guards be placed around the tomb so that His followers could not take His body and claim that He had risen from the dead (see Mt. 27:64). Mary also believed that someone had carried off the body of Jesus.

Our hope is found in a greater revelation of Jesus Christ. Mary followed Jesus for at least a couple of years, but despite her closeness to Him, she was hopeless.

She had been delivered of seven devils—she was still hopeless.

She had heard the teaching—she was still hopeless.

She had seen countless miracles—she was still hopeless.

She was at the foot of the cross when Jesus spoke—she was still hopeless.

She saw an empty tomb—she was still hopeless.

She saw the angels—she was still hopeless.

None of it made sense to her. It was not real; it was not personal. She remained, despite the great teaching and deliverance, ignorant of the truth of Jesus and in her despair. She was hopeless because she hoped *for* something less than the risen Christ. It isn't wrong to hope *for* something, but our hope must be *in* God Himself. We can hope for healing, but healing cannot be our hope. We can hope for financial security, but financial security cannot be our hope. Our hope is in the character of a good and faithful God, in a risen and powerful LORD.

It is not what we know—it is not what we see in other lives or in miracles—but our personal revelation of Jesus and the experiencing of His personal intimacy that heals us from hopelessness. "And now, Lord, for what do I wait? My hope is in You" (Ps. 39:7).

It is here where Jesus and the grace of God become real to us. This is where we bring our lives under the reality of His presence. This is where we turn the corner in our faith and experience the dynamic reality of our lives in Christ. This was the place where Mary's personal knowledge of Jesus went from Lord to her personal LORD.

As we turn toward God, we see Him as He is and purify ourselves from what is not real. "And everyone who has this hope fixed on Him purifies himself, just as He is pure" (1 Jn. 3:3). The character of God is the collateral of our hope. We have cause to hope even in the bleakest of circumstances, even if things don't work out to our understanding. Why? Because in the end God is good. In eternity He will be glorified in our defeats and failures as much as or more than in our apparent triumphs.

For those living under the influence of hopelessness, this is an invitation from the living God to turn away from staring into the emptiness and turn toward Him. He is here, behind you even now, speaking your name.

(See *Altars of the Heart Personal Ministry Guide*)

Getting the Picture

How does the picture of Mary staring into the empty tomb compare with your life? When do you feel cursed, doomed, defeated, resigned, pessimistic, negative, disappointed, empty, depressed, or anything like these?

Can you describe a recent time when you felt the things described above? Write a brief description in the picture frame. Before you begin to write, acknowledge the presence and involvement of God through prayer. Do not proceed until you have bathed in prayer and His presence. Declare the intention of the Lord to bring you truth and healing and forbid any lies or interference from unclean spirits.

_____

_____

_____

_____

Describe what you were feeling in that recent event.

_____

_____

_____

Now, pray that the Lord would lead you to the source of those feelings. Ask Him to take you by the hand and lead you to a memory that feels like the recent event you described. Describe the memory picture in the frame below as you did with the recent event. (Note that there may be more than one. Try to find the oldest memory.)

_____

_____

_____

_____

Ask the Lord to fill the memory with His presence. Describe how you experience the presence of God in that picture.

_____

_____

_____

_____

Once you have begun to experience the presence of God, ask yourself the following questions. What are you feeling as you look at this memory frame? Why do you feel that way? What did you believe about that event? What does the Lord seem to be telling you about the truth of that situation?

What are you feeling as you look at this memory frame? Why do you feel that way? What did you believe about that event? Now pray for the Lord to show you what is true.

I believed: _____

But the truth is: _____

Cleaning the House: Forgive, release as led of the Spirit.

What was true in the past is true in the present and will be God's promise to you in the future. Now revisit the present situation you cited at the beginning of this exercise. How do you see it now in light of what God has shown you?

What was true in the past? _____

What is true in the present? _____

What is God's promise to you for the future? _____

Why are you in despair, O my soul? And why have you become disturbed within me? Hope in God, for I shall again praise Him for the help of His presence (Psalm 42:5).

Part III

WALKING IN THE TRUTH

Chapter Thirteen

TO BE CONTINUED...

The Lord your God will clear away these nations before you lit-
tle by little; you will not be able to put an end to them quickly,
for the wild beasts would grow too numerous for you
(Deuteronomy 7:22).

The healing work has begun in you. Now you must walk through
and take possession of your inheritance "little by little." The Lord has led
you to the source of your pain and brought truth, order, and peace to your
heart. He has replaced lies with truth and given you a new awareness of
His presence and His loving intentions toward you. But the healing work
goes on—it is *to be continued.*

Our healing continues as we walk closer to the Lord and find more
Truth—more of Jesus Christ—more of the abundant life He purchased
for us. All healing and truth converge at the cross of Christ. Our healing
now continues to pervade every aspect of our lives to dethrone every fear
and every thought that exalts itself against the knowledge (truth) of God.
We take every thought captive as we obey and turn toward the voice of
the One who loves and accepts us (see 2 Cor. 10:3-5).

New Ruts

Roy Kreider, my mentor in inner healing, taught me that we tend to
live in ruts worn by habits and routine. Roy, who grew up in Lancaster
County, Pennsylvania, used the image of a horse-drawn wagon returning
to the barn at the end of the day. When a wagon has been on the same
path many times, it digs deep ruts in the dirt. The well-worn ruts in the
earth then provide a kind of guide or track that guide the wheels of the
wagon. As long as the farmer can get the wagon in the ruts, he can just
slap the horses on the rump, send them on their way to the barn, and not
even have to drive the wagon.

159

You and I have worn ruts in the landscape of our minds and hearts. There are patterns established in our lives and understanding that carry us to the barn, so to speak. Even when we have received truth and healing, those ruts are still there and our lives run into them. The solution is to continue to walk—to live—new truths and follow a new path that always leads us to Jesus.

We quoted the prophet Isaiah in an early chapter where he said, "You will see your teacher with your own eyes, and you will hear a voice say, 'This is the way; turn around and walk here' " (Is. 30:20b-21 NLT). As you journeyed through this book, you did indeed meet your Teacher and hear His voice. His voice has caused you to turn in a new direction—to repent from old thinking and ruts and find the true way to Him and healing. Now that you have heard and turned toward the presence of the Lord Jesus, you must *continue* to walk toward Him.

Jesus told those who followed Him to continue to walk in the new paths He had provided for them—paths that would lead to more and more freedom.

So Jesus was saying to those Jews who had believed Him, "If you continue in My word, then you are truly disciples of Mine; and you will know the truth, and the truth will make you free" (John 8:31-32).

Jesus said that it was not enough to hear the truth; we need to continue to walk it out, to make it part of our lives. Even when we have heard the truth and believed it, we can still fall into the familiar ruts and patterns that have carried us through life. It is as we continue to walk in the truth He speaks to us do we come to know it by experience and wear new ruts of righteousness in our lives that lead us to Him.

All healing and all truth converge at the cross of Christ. It was at the cross that all the lies and ruts of Eden's fall were eliminated and a new path provided. The way of the cross leads to intimacy with God Himself through the atoning work of Christ. If separation from the presence of God is the root of all emotional pain—and it is—then union with God in Christ is the healing for it. In His presence there is fullness of joy...healing...peace...abundant life.

As we close this book, I want to give you some new and "righteous ruts" to follow. Allow the truth of the Word to lead you to the fount of all healing: Jesus Christ. Read these words in the presence of God and follow the Teacher's voice to the source. When you are afraid, or whenever your wheels seem to find those old ruts that were so automatic, declare these truths and allow yourself to see them unfold before your lives. You have new promises in the presence of Jesus Christ.

The Healing Truth

- ### Fear—You Are Not Alone.

  Behold, I am with you and will keep you wherever you go, and will bring you back to this land; for I will not leave you until I have done what I have promised you (Genesis 28:15).

  Be strong and courageous, do not be afraid or tremble at them, for the Lord your God is the one who goes with you. He will not fail you or forsake you (Deuteronomy 31:6).

  Have I not commanded you? Be strong and courageous! Do not tremble or be dismayed, for the Lord your God is with you wherever you go (Joshua 1:9).

  The Lord of hosts is with us; the God of Jacob is our stronghold (Psalm 46:7).

  Be strong and courageous, do not fear or be dismayed because of the king of Assyria nor because of all the horde that is with him; for the one with us is greater than the one with him (2 Chronicles 32:7).

  But now, thus says the Lord, your Creator, O Jacob, and He who formed you, O Israel, "Do not fear, for I have redeemed you; I have called you by name; you are Mine! When you pass through the waters, I will be with you; and through the rivers, they will not overflow you. When you walk through the fire, you will not be scorched, nor will the flame burn you" (Isaiah 43:1-2).

- ### Rejection—You Are Accepted in Christ.

  They will say of Me, "Only in the Lord are righteousness and strength." Men will come to Him, and all who were angry at

Him will be put to shame. In the Lord all the offspring of Israel will be justified and will glory (Isaiah 45:24-25).

In His days Judah will be saved, and Israel will dwell securely; and this is His name by which He will be called, "The Lord our righteousness" (Jeremiah 23:6).

For all have sinned and fall short of the glory of God, being justified as a gift by His grace through the redemption which is in Christ Jesus (Romans 3:23-24).

For the kingdom of God is not eating and drinking, but righteousness and peace and joy in the Holy Spirit. For he who in this way serves Christ is acceptable to God and approved by men (Romans 14:17-18).

Having predestined us to adoption as sons by Jesus Christ to Himself, according to the good pleasure of His will, to the praise of the glory of His grace, by which He has made us accepted in the Beloved (Ephesians 1:5-6 NKJ).

- ***Worthlessness—You Are Approved in Christ, Handmade and Precious.***

God created man in His own image, in the image of God He created him; male and female He created them (Genesis 1:27).

Know that the Lord Himself is God; it is He who has made us, and not we ourselves; we are His people and the sheep of His pasture (Psalm 100:3).

Your hands made me and fashioned me; give me understanding, that I may learn Your commandments (Psalm 119:73).

For You formed my inward parts; You wove me in my mother's womb. I will give thanks to You, for I am fearfully and wonderfully made; wonderful are Your works, and my soul knows it very well (Psalm 139:13-14).

The people whom I formed for Myself will declare My praise (Isaiah 43:21).

But by the grace of God I am what I am... (1 Corinthians 15:10).

Therefore if anyone is in Christ, he is a new creature; the old things passed away; behold, new things have come (2 Corinthians 5:17).

For we are His workmanship, created in Christ Jesus for good works, which God prepared beforehand so that we would walk in them (Ephesians 2:10).

Do not lie to one another, since you laid aside the old self with its evil practices, and have put on the new self who is being renewed to a true knowledge according to the image of the One who created him (Colossians 3:9-10).

- ***Shame—You Are Clothed with Christ.***

How blessed is he whose transgression is forgiven, whose sin is covered! (Psalm 32:1)

For all of you who were baptized into Christ have clothed yourselves with Christ (Galatians 3:27).

I will rejoice greatly in the Lord, my soul will exult in my God; for He has clothed me with garments of salvation, He has wrapped me with a robe of righteousness (Isaiah 61:10a).

But put on the Lord Jesus Christ, and make no provision for the flesh in regard to its lusts (Romans 13:14).

- ***Insecurity—You Are Safe in Christ.***

The eternal God is a dwelling place, and underneath are the everlasting arms (Deuteronomy 33:27a).

O Lord, how my adversaries have increased! Many are rising up against me. Many are saying of my soul, "There is no deliverance for him in God." Selah. But You, O Lord, are a shield about me, my glory, and the One who lifts my head (Psalm 3:1-3).

Many are the sorrows of the wicked, but he who trusts in the Lord, lovingkindness shall surround him (Psalm 32:10).

The angel of the Lord encamps around those who fear Him, and rescues them (Psalm 34:7).

*The Lord is your **keeper**; the Lord is your shade on your right hand. The sun will not smite you by day, nor the moon by night. The Lord will **protect** you from all evil; He will **keep** your soul. The Lord will **guard** your going out and your coming in from this time forth and forever* (Psalm 121:5-8).

Those who trust in the Lord are as Mount Zion, which cannot be moved but abides forever. As the mountains surround Jerusalem, so the Lord surrounds His people from this time forth and forever (Psalm 125:1-2).

My sheep hear My voice, and I know them, and they follow Me; and I give eternal life to them, and they will never perish; and no one will snatch them out of My hand. My Father, who has given them to Me, is greater than all; and no one is able to snatch them out of the Father's hand (John 10:27-29).

- **Defilement—You Are Restored in Christ.**

O God, restore us and cause Your face to shine upon us, and we will be saved (Psalm 80:3).

"For I will restore you to health and I will heal you of your wounds," declares the Lord, "Because they have called you an outcast, saying: 'It is Zion; no one cares for her'" (Jeremiah 30:17).

"Then I passed by you and saw you, and behold, you were at the time for love; so I spread My skirt over you and covered your nakedness. I also swore to you and entered into a covenant with you so that you became Mine," declares the Lord God (Ezekiel 16:8).

Also I will restore the captivity of My people Israel, and they will rebuild the ruined cities and live in them; they will also plant vineyards and drink their wine, and make gardens and eat their fruit (Amos 9:14).

For the Lord will restore the splendor of Jacob like the splendor of Israel, even though devastators have devastated them and destroyed their vine branches (Nahum 2:2).

- **Hopelessness—You Have a Living Hope in Christ.**

  O Israel, hope in the Lord; for with the Lord there is lovingkindness, and with Him is abundant redemption (Psalm 130:7).

  For in hope we have been saved, but hope that is seen is not hope; for who hopes for what he already sees? But if we hope for what we do not see, with perseverance we wait eagerly for it (Romans 8:24-25).

  Blessed be the God and Father of our Lord Jesus Christ, who according to His great mercy has caused us to be born again to a living hope through the resurrection of Jesus Christ from the dead, to obtain an inheritance which is imperishable and undefiled and will not fade away, reserved in heaven for you, who are protected by the power of God through faith for a salvation ready to be revealed in the last time (1 Peter 1:3-5).

  Therefore, prepare your minds for action, keep sober in spirit, fix your hope completely on the grace to be brought to you at the revelation of Jesus Christ (1 Peter 1:13).

  And everyone who has this hope fixed on Him purifies himself, just as He is pure (1 John 3:3).

There are many other Scriptures that could be added to these. I urge you to search them out. Read His words and allow them to draw you into His presence. Hear His voice and know Him.

The Beginning...

"For I am confident of this very thing, that He who began a good work in you will perfect it until the day of Christ Jesus" (Phil. 1:6). He has begun this work and drawn you into His presence to unveil His heart for you—to speak of His love for you. Continue in His Word and His love, listening for the sound of a gentle stilling as He speaks truth and peace to your heart. I encourage you to read and reread this book many times. Wear it out. Weep into it. Write down what the Lord speaks to you. He is speaking to you, even now, as you read these words. He is leading you to a new place of abundant, overflowing life in His presence.

Beloved, I whisper softly this invitation to you. I am thinking of you and praying for you as I echo these words spoken so long ago and that are still true for you today:

> *...the Lord longs to pour out His healing oil on you, to be gracious to you; He waits on high to demonstrate His intimate love for you. The Lord Himself will bless and reward your longing for Him with His presence* (Isaiah 30:18, paraphrased).

AMEN—Let it be so in Christ Jesus!

REFERENCES

Biblesoft's New Exhaustive Strong's Numbers and Concordance with Expanded Greek-Hebrew Dictionary. 1994. Biblesoft and International Bible Translators, Inc.

Crabb, Larry. 1977. *Effective Biblical Counseling*. Grand Rapids, MI: Zondervan Publishing House.

Flynn, Mike, and Doug Gregg. 1993. *Inner Healing*. Downers Grove, IL: Intervarsity Press.

Kraft, Charles H. 1993. *Deep Wounds, Deep Healing*. Ann Arbor, MI: Servant Pub.

Long, Brad, and Cindy Strickler. 2001. *Let Jesus Heal Your Hidden Wounds*. Grand Rapids, MI: Chosen Books.

Petersen, Alice; Gary Sweeten; and Dorothy Faye Geverdt. 1990. "Renewing Mind." *Rational Christian Thinking*. Cincinnati: Equipping Ministries Int'l.

Sandford, John, and Paula Sandford. 1985. *Healing the Wounded Spirit*. Tulsa, OK: Victory House, Inc.

Sandford, John Loren, and Mark Sandford. 1992. *A Comprehensive Guide to Deliverance and Healing*. Grand Rapids, MI: Chosen Books.

Seamands, David A. 1985. *Healing of Memories*. Colorado Springs, CO: Chariot Victor Pub.

Smith, Edward M. 2002. *Beyond Tolerable Recovery*. Campbellsville, KY: Family Care Pub.

MINISTRY INFORMATION

The mission of Grace and Truth Fellowship, Inc., is to transform local churches into healing centers. Serving as president of this ministry, Thom Gardner is available as a speaker/teacher for seminars, conferences, or other extended meetings. Grace and Truth Fellowship, Inc., also offers the *Altars of the Heart Ministry Training Seminar* to equip the local church to bring healing to wounded hearts. The purpose of the seminar is to help the participants find personal freedom through confrontation of their own past wounds, and then equip them to bring healing to others.

The *Altars of the Heart Ministry Training Seminar* is a three-day seminar that covers the material in this book and offers instruction and practice in the facilitation of this approach to healing wounded hearts. Our goal is to multiply, rather than monopolize, this approach to the ministry of inner healing.

If you are interested in arranging an *Altars of the Heart Ministry Training Seminar*, contact Grace and Truth Fellowship, Inc., at 717-263-6869, or see our web site at www.graceandtruth.us.

THOM GARDNER

Altars of the Heart and
Altars of the Heart Personal Ministry Guide

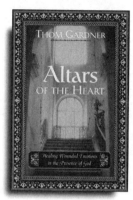

0-7684-3009-7

0-7684-3020-8

Altars of the Heart is a living and healing picture that wraps powerful expositions of the Word around the lives of real people. The compelling hope of the book flows from the hearts of many people who have been healed from emotional pain by the presence of the Lord.

Gardner exposes negative emotions such as fear, rejection, worthlessness, shame, insecurity, defilement, and hopelessness that prevent us from living in the grace and peace God intends for us. You will walk through a gentle process, uncovering lies embedded in your emotional wounds and discovering peace and truth in the presence of the Living Christ. *Altars of the Heart* will bring you to a new sense of intimate closeness with God as it leads you to a healing place in the heart of God.

171

Additional copies of this book and other
book titles from DESTINY IMAGE are
available at your local bookstore.

For a complete list of our titles,
visit us at www.destinyimage.com
Send a request for a catalog to:

Destiny Image® Publishers, Inc.

P.O. Box 310

Shippensburg, PA 17257-0310

*"Speaking to the Purposes of God for This
Generation and for the Generations to Come"*